Here's What People Are Saying about
Coaching for Teamwork

"Vince Lombardi, in clear, no-nonsense language has written a masterful treatise on what it takes to achieve excellence whether you are a football coach, a businessman, or a valued member of your community. Just as I will recommend this book to our players, to our coaches, and to everyone in the Buffalo Bills organization, I recommend it, also, to everyone who has a desire to realize their full potential."

—*Marv Levy*, Head Coach, Buffalo Bills

"Vince Lombardi has captured the essence of the modern workplace and workforce. The rules about structure, responsibility, technology, communication have changed—and the rules protecting companies from competition are being eliminated. So Vince points out, the coach that can put together the team will be the winner of the future."

**—*Frederic H. Betrand*, Chairman of the Board
and Chief Executive Officer
Vermont National Life Insurance Company**

"A 'must read' where teamwork and organizational results are essential. Vince has captured and effectively packaged the 'teamwork magic' his father perfected. Well researched . . . direct . . . hard hitting!"

**—*James F. Hennig*, Ph.D
1995-96 President, National Speakers Association**

"Vince Lombardi, like his father before him, has searched all his life for the path to achievement. He has digested, refined and added to his father's thoughts. Though their paths may differ, the end result is the same—achievement."

—*Jerry Kramer*, **Green Bay Packers, 1958-1969**
Author, with Dick Schaap, of *Instant Replay,*
Farewell to Football, Lombardi: Winning is
the Only Thing **and** *Distant Replay*

"This book, *Coaching for Teamwork*, highlights and demonstrates the concepts of coaching and teamwork that are required to be a successful leader in today's competitive business environment. Creating and establishing a vision and then employing the concept of 'running to win' will provide success. I highly recommend this book to all managers as a reference to provide focus for growth and victory."

—*R. W. Tarrant*, **Chairman, CEO, President**
Flow International Corporation

". . . thought provoking . . . a good tool to reevaluate your management skills, goals and vision. Provides an opportunity to reflect on the ever-changing business environment and helps establish a blueprint that will take you into the 21st century."

—*John E. Beake*, **General Manager**
Denver Broncos Football Club

"Vince Lombardi is his father's son and more, taking those principles and practices by which his father led the Green Bay Packers to unparalleled football success and expanding them in this thoroughly researched and creatively presented book to apply to all of us whether we seek the individual, company or corporate fulfillment that is success."

—*W. C. Heinz*, **Author of** *The Professional, The Surgeon,*
and with Vince Lombardi, *Run To Daylight*

Coaching for Teamwork

Winning Concepts for Business in the Twenty-First Century

Coaching for Teamwork

Winning Concepts for Business in the Twenty-First Century

Vince Lombardi

Reinforcement Press
2820 122nd Place, NE
Bellevue, WA 98005

Although the author and publisher have made every effort to ensure the accuracy and completeness of information contained in this book, we assume no responsibility for errors, inaccuracies, omissions, or any inconsistency herein. Any slights of people, places, or organizations are unintentional.

First printing 1996

ISBN 0-9647810-0-X

LCCN 95-71467

Editing, design, typesetting, and printing services provided by About Books, Inc., 425 Cedar Street, Buena Vista, CO 81211, 800-548-1876.

ATTENTION CORPORATIONS, UNIVERSITIES, COLLEGES, AND PROFESSIONAL ORGANIZATIONS: Quantity discounts are available on bulk purchases of this book for educational purposes or fund raising. Special books or book excerpts can also be created to fit specific needs. For information, please contact Reinforcement Press, 2820 122nd Place NE, Bellevue WA 98005, or phone 1-800-736-6196.

Table of Contents

Now this is the law of the jungle
As old and as true as the sky;
And the wolf that keeps it may prosper
And the wolf that shall break it must die.
As the creeper that circles the tree trunk,
The law runneth forward and back
The strength of the pack is the wolf,
And the strength of the wolf is the pack.

—Rudyard Kipling

Introduction

Many American companies are discovering what may be the productivity breakthrough of the 1990s. Call the still controversial innovation a self-managed team, a cross functional team, a high performance team, or to coin a phrase, a superteam. No matter what your business, these teams are the wave of the future.

—Jerry Junkins

Teamwork is a hot topic today. Championships are won with it. Productivity is increased with it. Quality is improved with it. *Teams* and *teamwork* are revolutionizing how we do business in America and around the world. We don't have to look far to find an example of the benefits and rewards of teamwork—no farther than the joint allied effort to win the Gulf War, and in particular the role American troops played in that winning effort. The Gulf War, managed brilliantly and won with startling brevity, was a triumph of teamwork—and a dramatic departure from the experience of American troops in their last great test, Vietnam.

In Vietnam, interservice rivalry hampered action in the field. Distrust between officers and enlisted men was widespread, performance at all

1

levels was uneven, and the chain of command was often twisted by micromanagement.

After the Vietnam war, American military leaders made a fundamental change in their approach to the team concept, and called it *integrated cooperation.* The contrast was dramatic, and of course, so were the results. In Vietnam top commanders, including the President, rearranged the battlefield and selected the targets. Remember Tonkin Bay? The mining of Haiphong harbor?

In the Gulf War, field officers were trusted to make their own decisions. One field commander was quoted as saying, "What General Schwartzkopf did was give his commanders a mission and say 'go do it,' and you didn't hear from him after that. That's all any commander can ask for." That's all anyone can ask for.

How did the American military achieve this success? The same way you bring this kind of success to your organization. By *coaching for teamwork.*

A book on coaching for teamwork is an ambitious project. But this book can provide you with the tools you need to build a high-performance team within your organization. Ken Blanchard, coauthor of *The One Minute Manager*, says, "We teach what we need to learn." That's it for me. I've been part of many different teams in the private and public sector, and it has been part of my mission to analyze successful organizations.

Specifically, *what do winning teams do and how do they do it?*

I've distilled my observations with those of others and simplified them into easily understood concepts. My intention is to present these concepts to you in a straightforward manner, free of the jargon often encountered in books of this kind. (I've tried to keep words like paradigm, empowerment, functional boundaries, core processes, and job enrichment to an absolute minimum.) A few personal words. My father was one of the great coaches of the modern football era—yes, *that* Vince Lombardi. His Green Bay Packers set a standard of excellence rarely approached in the history of the National Football League. You probably know how good the Packers were; you may not be aware just how bad they had been. The year before my father took over, the Packers had a record of one win, ten losses, and a tie. They were inept enough to give Red Smith, the great sportswriter, a chance to coin one of the enduring phrases of his craft. Smith wrote that the Packers of 1958 "overwhelmed one, underwhelmed ten and whelmed one."

Yet in 1960, in my father's second year in Green Bay, the Packers played for the World Championship. They lost that game, but they never lost another championship game. Over the next seven years they won five NFL Championships, three in a row, including the first two Super Bowls. Not only is that a study in how to *attain* a goal, it's a study in how to *maintain* a goal. If you have experienced some success, you know it's far tougher to stay on top than it is to get to the top.

History is full of coaches who have won one championship and business leaders who have a good quarter or a good year. The mark of a great coach, a great team, or a great businessperson is to win year after year, time after time after time.

How do you take a group of people, full of doubt and tentative in their performance, and transform them into a team of champions? It's a good question and the answer to it forms the spine of this book. Because whether you're trying to build a winning football team, a winning sales force, or a winning production team—or trying to take your organization from where it is today to where you want it to be—the principles are essentially the same.

I watched those principles put into action from a ringside seat. From eighth grade until I was out of college I went to training camp with my father—first with the New York Giants, where he was an assistant coach, and then with the Packers. And even before that, I hung around the practice field at West Point, where my father was an assistant coach for the Army team.

I didn't have this book in mind during those times, but in the years since, I've had a lot of "aha" feelings as I related current observations back to those practice field experiences. So that was where I began to absorb the principles of good leadership—although I didn't realize it at the time.

I saw my father lead with encouragement and lead with criticism. I saw him yell at players and figuratively undress them in front of their teammates. Often it would embarrass me—because as I got older many of these players were my friends. Some of those players would bounce back and make that second effort to succeed; some wouldn't. Those who didn't were soon gone. Of course, if my father came across a player with talent, who couldn't handle being yelled at, he would find a different way to motivate him.

Over my 53 years I have had a few coaches myself, in and out of sports. Some were better than others. Some had energy and enthusiasm. Some others were negative, demeaning and incompetent. Two in particular I would have followed anywhere, because at the time they believed in me more than I believed in myself. I learned from *all* of them.

- I learned that when a leader assumes a new job she had better bring a recognized expertise or a positive reputation. Otherwise people will cut the new leader little or no slack.

- I learned that leaders listen.
- I learned that leaders don't criticize every mistake. They let people learn from their mistakes. As an employee I felt worse about my mistakes than my boss did.
- I learned that leaders delegate and assume the job will get done. The able leaders I knew didn't constantly look over my shoulder, yet they were available if I had a question.
- I learned that the best leaders are those with willing followers.
- I learned that leaders understand loyalty rests with the troops, not the higher-ups. Leaders earned my loyalty by going to bat for me.

And finally, I've been a manager, a leader, and a coach. I've had people look to me for answers when I didn't have them. I've needed to move people to action when I had difficulty motivating myself. I've delegated and held my breath. I found out the hard way that as a leader I wasn't a very good listener. Finally, I learned that the real satisfaction in being a leader is mentoring people and helping them grow. These were the most valuable lessons of all.

A major premise for this book is that there are parallels between business and team sports, particularly football, and there are lessons from team sports—coaching and team building—that people in business can learn and apply. Consequently, you will find numerous references to sports throughout this book.

I believe the parallels between team sports and business are valid. The principles of building a winning football team and building a successful business enterprise are similar. When 311 business executives were asked to list the five people who most often influenced their

Business is a combination of war and sport.
—Andre Maurois

workplace decisions, two were Jimmy Johnson, then coach of the Dallas Cowboys, and Pat Riley, then coach of the New York Knicks. (As reported in the the the March 6, 1994 edition of the *New York Times*)

There are those who point out that in sports you have a winner and a loser and this breeds a scarcity mentality that's counterproductive in a business context. I agree. *In business everyone can win.* If the enterprise is successful, everyone can benefit: the owner/shareholders, the customer, management, employees, and suppliers. Once you get beyond this point, the parallels between team sports and business are demonstrable and striking.

The team concept in this book relates to performing better when we are cooperating with other members of the team as opposed to trying to beat some other team.

The sharpest opportunities to study group dynamics under stressful conditions are offered by warfare and team sports, particularly football. And football is a lot safer to study than war. Football is a violent game; no other team sport makes comparable demands on coaches and players. Football is a game of lessons; lessons a manager and a leader can apply to his or her business world. My father was quoted as saying, *"Winning isn't everything, it's the only thing."* He took a lot of criticism for that statement because people misapplied it. Winning shouldn't be everything for ten-year-old little leaguers or high school football players. But my father wasn't talking about those levels of competition. In the context of pro sports and the business world, winning *is* everything. As a leader, you are judged—and your compensation is based—on the results you achieve and the goals you reach.

Your success needn't be at the expense of some other individual or company. Nevertheless, the payoff in business, in sports, and in life

One of my lawyers told me to read the sports section first every morning. It talks of mankind's successes, while other parts of the paper talk about mankind's problems or failures.
—Michael Milken

Sports serve society by providing vivid examples of excellence.
—George Will

Football is a great deal like life in that it teaches that work, sacrifice, perseverance, competitive drive, selflessness and respect for authority is the price that each and every one of us must pay to achieve any goal that is worthwhile.
—Vincent T. Lombardi

comes from results—in other words, winning. Your definition of winning may differ from my definition, but that doesn't diminish the parallels between team sports and business.

Successful coaches communicate, organize, and lead. They engender within the organization the resiliency and mental toughness to respond quickly and decisively to a new situation every game. The techniques, strategies, tactics, and lessons of team sports can be learned by business people; they can be applied to their advantage and to the benefit of their organization. These lessons will be developed in this book.

Finally, a brief word on the liberal use of quotations in this book. I like quotations. They entertain, they provoke, and they add authority to just about anything. Quotations often illustrate a point I want to make. Don't just breeze by these quotes. They are an integral part of the book.

We want to perfect ourselves so that we can win with less struggle and increasing ease, but the strange thing is that it's not the easy wins we ostensibly seek, but rather the difficult struggles to which we really look forward.
—Vincent T. Lombardi

I quote others only the better to express myself.
—Herbert Gardner

The wisdom of the wise and the experience of the ages are perpetuated by quotes.
—Benjamin Disraeli

Coaching for Teamwork

Never doubt that a small group of thoughtful, committed people can change the world. Indeed, it is the only thing that ever has.

—Margaret Mead

The challenges in our path as we approach the next millennium loom over the business world like a Himalayan mountain—increased global competition, deregulation, takeovers and mergers, downsizing, rapid technological change, and the information explosion.

But as imposing as they are, in one sense these challenges are healthy. They have forced us to focus on a better way of doing things: the concepts of *teamwork* and *coaching for teamwork.*

Teamwork is more than a catchword. It is the key to organizational success in the 1990s and into the 21st century. If you are a business owner, a manager, or an organizational leader and you are serious about staying competitive, *teamwork* holds the key.

If you understand that to increase productivity and improve quality, new thinking and new skills are called for; and if you agree that your most powerful resource is the group of people

The pace of change in the Nineties will make the Eighties look like a picnic, a walk in the park. Competition will be relentless. The bar of excellence in everything we do will be raised every day.

—Jack Welch

9

People acting together as a group can accomplish things which no individual acting alone could ever hope to bring about.
                —Franklin D. Roosevelt

It is of course a trite observation to say we live in a period of transition; many people have said this many times. Adam may well have made the remark to Eve on leaving the Garden of Eden.
                —Harold McMillan

who are working for you right now, then you must understand what can unlock their full potential for your organization—*teamwork*.

Are you reorganizing or reengineering? Downsizing and empowering your people? Are you implementing Total Quality Management? The bedrock foundation for any and all of these changes is *teamwork*, the very difficult task of getting your people first to think as a team, and then act as a team.

Why this interest in teamwork? Many commentators, including Tom Peters in his book *Thriving On Chaos*, say we are witnessing nothing less cataclysmic than the demise of large organizations. These times of change and transition impose a burden of creativity that large, top-heavy organizations are unable to sustain.

Big organizations may lack the speed and flexibility to ensure survival. Big corporations may lack the agility to be fast and aggressive and at the same time make mistakes and quickly cut their losses. But teams can change direction quickly. Teams, by definition, are not large and by design are not cumbersome.

Sheer size can be a disadvantage, and the day may soon come when a large organization will find itself following the career path of the dinosaurs, and for the same reason.

Pat Riley, coach of the Miami Heat, extols the advantages inherent in the small size of an athletic team in his book *The Winner Within*. Athletic teams see one another and work together on a daily basis. Because it plays almost every day or every week, he says, the athletic team not only has a built-in monitor of its performance, but can easily keep a watchful finger on the pulse of its own morale. If a working unit is not compact enough to do these things for itself, it's probably too big to compete in today's business environment.

In years past a manager drew his real

authority from the special knowledge and information flowing to him, and only to him. But today, the shoulders of the information highway are littered with data to be read by anyone in the corporate world. The paper trail of the past has given way to an electronic communication flood—PCs, E-mail, modems, and cellular phones—that has inundated the workplace. The manager is no longer the keeper of the knowledge base, and there is too much information for a manager to control, anyway. John Naisbitt's *Megatrends* made it popular to say we're in the information age. It would be more accurate to say we're in the information explosion. And it isn't just the mountain of facts, data, and information; it's the vast distribution of that information to people who in another time would have had to wait to learn from a manager what today they can learn for themselves. The *New York Sunday Times* contains more data, facts, and information than was available in a lifetime just 50 years ago!

The spread of information technology has made the world of business smaller, faster and fiercely competitive.

- The pony express delivered a letter in 8 days
- The airplane cut delivery to 6 days
- Jet aircraft delivered the letter in 3 days
- Federal Express will get the letter there overnight
- A fax machine will deliver the letter in 5 seconds

What does it all mean? It means that top-down management doesn't work. A one-way information flow down the organizational chart is out of date and unresponsive to today's workforce. It means you maximize your company's chances for success by adopting the team approach to your workplace.

The world is moving so fast these days that the man who says it can't be done is generally interrupted by someone doing it.
—Elbert Hubbard

The secret is to work less as individuals and more as a team. As a coach I play not my eleven best, but my best eleven.
  —Knute Rockne

Teamwork is the primary ingredient of success.
  —Vincent T. Lombardi

Peter Drucker, a popular and prolific management theorist, is quoted as saying:

"Knowledge workers still need a superior . . . but knowledge work itself knows no hierarchy, for there are no 'higher' and 'lower' knowledges. Knowledge is either relevant to a given task or irrelevant to it. The task decides; not the name, the age, or the budget of the discipline, or the rank of the individual plying it. Knowledge, therefore, has to be organized as a team in which the task decides who is in charge, when, for what, and for how long."

Today's business environment requires people to become entrepreneurial and manage their own work—which means taking full advantage of the vast body of knowledge and the communications equipment available to them that allows them to manage their own work. This results in flatter organizations with management functions being pushed farther down the organization chart. Consequently, people at the top must be more coach than manager. If both public and private institutions are going to prosper into the 21st century, *coaching for teamwork* must be a priority.

The team approach has already made successful inroads in a variety of settings—teams are being used with dramatic results in auto, aerospace, electronic equipment and electronics, food processing, paper, steel, and financial services. Some very big companies have employed teams to bring bulky operations down to a manageable size, among them General Electric, Boeing, Caterpillar, Champion International, Ford, Cummins, General Mills, Federal Express, 3M, Aetna Life and Casualty, and IDS.

Reports from these and other companies show that teams can quickly, aggressively, and creatively:

- Improve employee involvement and managerial support
- Give employees a sense of ownership and increase their commitment
- Increase focus on the customer and subsequent customer satisfaction
- Reduce labor costs and improve quality

Why a coach? Why not a manager? Why not a leader? Aren't these terms interchangeable? They are not. You manage capital equipment, you manage numbers and production. But if you attempt to *manage* people you may regret it; people don't like the idea of being "managed" today. It's the 1990s. I'm working for you, and you're "managing" me? It's just not going to work. People will not put up with being "managed" today. They may not literally quit on you, but they'll find ways to figuratively quit on you and they will certainly frustrate and defeat your efforts to "manage" them.

Bert was a competent, well-intentioned manager who had a weakness he thought was a strength. He felt he knew everyone's job as well as his own, and his managerial style included a willingness to tell everyone working for him how to do his or her job. Nor did Bert hesitate to tell people from other departments how to do their jobs. Bert's company was in disarray; his management technique was just one of many problems. When a new president was hired, he was greeted with a steady stream of people coming to his office, complaining of how difficult it was to work with Bert. The president came to realize he was spending an inordinate amount of time refereeing interoffice squabbles caused by Bert's management style. Ultimately Bert was terminated.

Do you see yourself as a leader? Fine. We need leaders today. My experience suggests that when things get difficult, leaders tend to take matters into their own hands. "Step aside, let me show you how to do this." "If you want things done right, you've got to do it yourself."

If you are this kind of leader, you may regard the success of the organization as a personal responsibility, a burden not to be shared with subordinates. The downside for this type of leadership is that your productivity will go down the drain; sooner or later, probably sooner, your people will quit trying to solve their problems. You've taught them that you'll be along shortly to do that for them. You've always done it in the past.

And just as quickly, company morale will flow down the same drain. Because while you solved the problem of the moment, you created a far more basic one: you undermined the confidence of your staff, and started people thinking along a very destructive line—"Doesn't she have any confidence in us?" "Doesn't he think we can do this job?"

When Jack took over the presidency of a company that was experiencing severe financial difficulty, Art, the former president, was still with the company as an advisor. It took Jack little time to realize that employee morale was at a low ebb, and he noted something else—the staff seemed to spend more time avoiding decisions than making them. Jack concluded that Art, while extremely able, was the reason. Art was harsh, outspoken, and very critical. If someone made a mistake Art didn't hesitate to tell them in no uncertain terms, and worse, he would take over the job until he felt it was being done right. Jack spent time trying to temper Art's leadership style, but quickly learned that Art took pride in how he handled things and saw no need to change. Jack recognized his mission demanded that he restore morale and get people to begin to accept accountability, and so when

To gain one's way is no escape from the responsibility for an inferior solution.
—Winston Churchill

persuasion didn't work, he began to move Art away from some of the key aspects of the company's operations.

Coaches, on the other hand, know they belong on the sidelines. Coaches know they can't play the game, know that only the players belong on the field of play, and that only players can actually win the game. Coaches don't do things, they see that things get done—things that ensure the players are totally prepared mentally and physically. Coaches seek to create an environment within which their players have the greatest opportunity to succeed. A coach knows she is only as good as her players, so her first priority is not to seek to personally duplicate the talents of her players, but rather to provide for them the things they can't provide for themselves—direction, authority and the freedom to do their jobs.

Consider: a coach knows the most important ingredient to winning are players—how they are recruited or drafted, how they are trained and motivated. No clear-thinking department head will see his people any differently.

It has always been a challenge to motivate people; changing rules in the workplace have made it a far more daunting task today. "My way or the highway" doesn't work on a consistent basis anymore, not on the practice field, not in the board room, not on the shop floor. Don't believe for a minute that coaches have any more control over their people than you do; indeed, coaches face problems in their profession that might intimidate any business-person. It is a rare corporate leader who is criticized and second-guessed in the media by his own people, as coaches are today. It is a rare shop foreman who encounters the challenge of managing people who are making more money than he is, and have more job security in the form of a guaranteed contract. Workplace diversity

The great leader is not the one in the spotlight. He's the one leading the applause.
—Anonymous

I have a theory that talent is very common. What's rare is the environment that allows talent to flourish.
—Mary Vinton Folberg

You're only as good as the people you hire.
—Ray Kroc

is both a goal and a challenge for business today. Coaches have been dealing with some aspects of this diversity for years.

Dick Vermeil quits the Philadelphia Eagles; Dan Issel walks away from the Denver Nuggets; Bill Walsh chooses to step down at Stanford; Bill McCartney packs it in at the University of Colorado; Don Nelson chooses not to continue coaching the Golden State Warriors. These incidents are all the result of the unique pressure coaches face.

Coaching has never been a secure profession. Coaches are fired every season for failing to succeed, usually because in some fashion they failed to react and respond to changes in their particular marketplace. Only in the last few years have business professionals experienced this same insecurity.

Accompanying this insecurity in business is the lack of loyalty in today's workforce. Turnover is high and people with talent are constantly on the move, following their own career path in search of greater rewards. Again, coaches have been dealing with constant turnover of personnel for a long time. College coaches experience a complete change in personnel every four or five years, and recent changes in free agency rules on the professional level have made coaches in football, baseball, and basketball acutely aware that a talent who is here today is likely to be gone to a better-paying competitor tomorrow.

The leader of the future is the coach. Listening, communicating, teaching, challenging, directing, delegating, motivating players on the field—while she remains on the sidelines. The coach is parent, teacher and referee, often at the same time.

Managing is like holding a dove in your hand. Squeeze it too hard and you kill it; not hard enough and it flies away.

—Tommy Lasorda

Successful coaches aren't punched out of a cookie cutter. Some coaches are organizers who delegate; they coach from a tower—Bear Bryant and Don James. Other coaches are hands on; they wear a headset and call the plays—Bill Parcells and Dan Reeves. Some are outwardly unemotional, like Tom Landry; and some are volatile, like Vince Lombardi. The lesson is that there's no single way to win, in sports or in your chosen field. The style you adopt, however, had better be *your* style, the way that's right for you, the way that confirms your credibility. You can't win using someone else's plays, style, or system. Your people are too smart for that; they'll see through you in a minute. I don't know who said this, but it certainly rings true: "You may fool those who work above you; you may fool those who work around you; but you rarely fool those who work under you."

In sports, whatever your coaching style, your players will support you *if you win*, but only as long as you win. Your players will disregard the little hurts, reach for new levels of energy, and push themselves to their limits if you give them the opportunity to improve their condition through success. Give them pride, purpose and meaning through the success of the team, and they will follow you anywhere. It has always been a source of wonder to me to see players rally to a coach's side as he or she is being fired for a losing record. Where was this kind of effort on game day?

The following is a letter my father wrote to each Packer player and his wife after the 1962 season. (Norm Masters was an offensive tackle on that team.)

January 4, 1963

Mr. and Mrs. Norm Masters
26029 Dover
Detroit, Michigan

Dear Norm and Jan,

Words can never express my gratitude for

Every man has a strong dose of egoism, pride, hardness and cunning. But all those things will be regarded as high qualities if he can make them the means to achieve great ends.

—Charles DeGaulle

your accomplishments of the past season. Our victory in the Championship Game was particularly pleasing since it meant so much to me personally.

I believe you realize now that success is much more difficult to live with than failure. I don't believe anyone realizes, except ourselves, the obstacles we had to face week after week. This, of course, made our season more gratifying.

I was extremely proud of our conduct during the Championship game. We never lost our poise under what were very trying conditions. The Giants tried to intimidate us physically, but in the final analysis, we were mentally tougher than they were and that same mental toughness made them crack.

Character is the perfectly disciplined will, and you are men of character. Our greatest glory was not in never falling, but in rising when we fell.

Best wishes to you both and remember, "There is no substitute for victory."

Sincerely,

Vince Lombardi
Head Coach and General Manager

1962 was a difficult year for the Packers. They were seeking to duplicate the championship they had won in 1961, never an easy assignment, and a number of injuries to key players didn't help. Yet Green Bay won 20 of the 21 games it played that year, separated from a perfect season only by a Thanksgiving Day defeat in Detroit. And the 21st game was a fitting climax.

The Packers traveled to New York City, where my father was born and raised, to play the New York Giants, his former team, for the NFL championship. On game day the temperature was in the low teens, and the winds were gusting between 30 and 40 miles per hour—so hard that a sideline bench was once blown 10 feet onto the field.

The field was like a parking lot, hard packed, filled with more pebbles than grass. And on this demanding day, in one of the most physically brutal games the NFL had ever seen in terms of the playing conditions and the caliber of play, the Packers defeated the Giants for the World Championship 16-7.

This, then, is more than a letter from a coach to his players. It is a letter from a teacher to his students.

> *Every encounter between a superior and a subordinate involves learning of some kind. When the boss gives an order, asks for a job to be done, reprimands, praises, conducts an appraisal review, deals with a mistake, holds a staff meeting, solves a problem, or takes any other action with subordinates, he is teaching.*
> *—Douglas McGregor*

Coaching, in sports, in the military, in the public or private sector, is first and foremost a teaching function. A coach must then address the next question: "Am I teaching the right thing?"

The thrust of my father's letter to his players after their triumph seeks to build and reinforce their self-esteem and self-confidence. They have just won the World Championship; almost immediately, their coach writes to them, expressing gratitude and pride in their achievement, emphasizing and reinforcing their mental toughness and character.

Distill all the tasks a coach must perform, all the things she must teach and instill within the team down to bedrock, and you will be left with this: confidence and self-esteem. Everything, all success and all achievement, flows directly from the level and depth of the self-esteem possessed by the team and its individual members. And the

They call it coaching, but it is teaching. You do not tell them it is so. You show them it is so.
—Vincent T. Lombardi

The most vital quality a soldier can possess is self-confidence.
—George S. Patton

essence of building self-esteem in an organization that has lacked it, is *change*, which means it won't be easy.

A great manager has a knack for making players think they're better than they think they are. Once you learn how good you really are, you never settle for playing less than your best.

—Reggie Jackson

People by their very nature resist change. We all prefer to remain where we are comfortable, where we can perform smoothly, with little tension or anxiety. It is a natural tendency to avoid situations that threaten our ability to handle matters effectively and be at our best. But the more we believe in ourselves—the higher our self-esteem—the more tension and anxiety we can endure to achieve team goals. There is a direct correlation between the level of self-esteem and the level of performance of both the individual and the team.

Think of it this way:

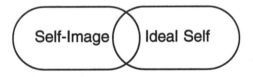

The *Self-Image* is the belief we have about ourselves. "This is the kind of person I am." "This is the kind of coach I am." "This is the kind of team player I am." The *Ideal Self* is the picture we have of that ideal person we want to become, and believe we can be. Where the Self-Image and the Ideal Self overlap, self-esteem and self-confidence are high. We see ourselves as we aspire to be. When Self-Image is far from the Ideal Self, the result is low self-esteem.

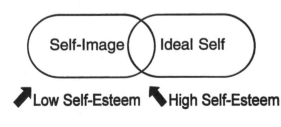

The coach's job, then, can be seen as this: to enlarge and expand the area of overlap between Self-Image and the Ideal Self. It's within this area of high self-esteem that individuals and teams consistently perform at their best. Teams, like individuals, have a self-image. The self-image of the team is a reflection of the collective self-image of all the players on the team.

I've got to make them believers.
—Vincent T. Lombardi

When I joined the Michigan Panthers of the United States Football League, they had just won the USFL championship, and the team's success continued the next year, when we made the playoffs. The following year, however, a league realignment found us merging with the Oakland Invaders, a team that had not enjoyed a lot of on-the-field success. I went to Oakland to operate the newly created team, and I brought with me two front office people from the Michigan team. Quite soon, I began to receive complaints from the Oakland staff. These fellows from Michigan, I was told, were demanding, pushy, and insisted on answers right away! I knew the caliber of these two people, and a little reflection revealed what was happening. The success of the Michigan team had given these men a self-image of themselves as winners. Their eagerness to get the job done and repeat their prior success simply made the Oakland people, who up to that time had no experience of success and no comparable self-image, uncomfortable.

What is the first thing a successful coach does when he takes over a losing team? He brings in some of his former players. He reaches out for players who have formed the habit of winning, know what it takes to win, and have a winning self-image. To be sure, the coach imports these players to upgrade the talent level of the team. But far more important, the coach wants these players, with the self-image of a winner, to begin to influence the poor self-image of their new team-mates. So critical is this need that I have known coaches to bring in players well past their prime, simply because they wear "The Ring"— the trophy that goes to Super Bowl winners. Athletes these days can afford many things, but a Super Bowl ring can be bought only with victory.

A team's success flows directly and measurably from the self-esteem and confidence of the team members. Belief in self determines the degree of commitment people are willing to bring to their job. There is a direct correlation between the level of self-esteem, confidence and belief in self and the team, and the resilience and mental toughness people apply to their efforts. The more deeply they believe in themselves and the team, the less likely they are to give up and quit in difficult circumstances. The flip side of this is that neither individuals nor teams can consistently outperform their level of confidence or self-esteem.

Teams need people with talent and ability, of course; the more talent and ability the team has, the greater likelihood of success. But the list of also-rans is full of contenders who forgot that it takes more than talent and ability to win on a consistent basis. Confidence and belief in your talent and ability to "get it done," to "make it happen"—these are the ingredients that transform contenders into champions.

This connection between belief and performance can be illustrated by what I call the *belief-performance cycle*:

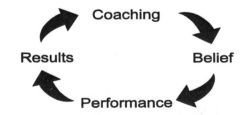

Coaching influences and builds belief. *Belief* directly impacts performance. *Performance* produces results. And *results*, positive or negative, provide the coach with another opportunity to

You cannot consistently perform in a manner which is inconsistent with the way you see yourself.

—Zig Ziglar

If you think you can, you can. And if you think you can't, you're right.

—Mary Kay Ash

teach and influence self-esteem, confidence, and belief. This cycle is endless. It goes around and around every day. Coaches must be constantly looking for opportunities to positively reinforce the confidence level of the team, because the simple truth is that the belief-performance cycle can be negative as well as positive.

We're all aware of professional sports teams who never seem able to put together a winning season. They try everything—a new coach, new general manager, new uniforms, a new slogan. They get the benefit of prime selections in the draft, and the first choice of the discards of their more successful rivals. Yet year after year the results are the same. Why? Because the team, try though it might, never reaches the heart of the problem; the defeatist beliefs and selfish attitudes in the locker room. As new players join the team, they are contaminated by these beliefs and attitudes. They bring no Super Bowl rings with them; instead, the "establishment" smoothly absorbs them, and poor work habits become ever more ingrained in the workplace.

Too often, teams find it easier to blame one person, the coach, than the many. And so the only true solution—getting rid of those people who are dragging the team down with their negative, defeatist attitude—is never tried. Another coach is dismissed, and the poison in the workplace continues.

Jim Mora in New Orleans and Jimmy Johnson in Dallas took over NFL teams that suffered from this defeatist attitude. To turn those teams around, they had only one course of action open to them. Clean house, get rid of everybody. That's what they did. By the time New Orleans and Dallas started winning, very few of the players who were there when Mora and Johnson took over had survived. Conversely, a number of years later, Barry Switzer took over the Dallas Cowboys from Jimmy Johnson. The Cowboys were Super Bowl

The basic problem that you face is developing a losing pattern. The most difficult thing in coaching is to overcome the feeling that you're going to lose.
—Tom Landry

Fire the Coach &
Keep the Same
players! Eek!
☹

Champions. They believed in themselves and in each other, they exuded confidence. Switzer made few changes and the team barely missed a beat.

Your team will experience negative results from time to time. You don't win them all. And when you suffer a setback, you can expect varied reactions from your people. Some will be committed and disciplined and won't allow a defeat to undermine their confidence. Many, however, don't possess this mental toughness, at least not yet. A defeat or setback will adversely affect their belief in themselves and the team, and in turn, negatively impact on the next performance.

In the midst of adversity, how do you combat negative feelings and beliefs? How does a coach prevent the downward spiral of defeat, loss of confidence, and more defeat? Through the *vision*, that clear precise picture of success that the coach has for his team. The vision is the *Ideal Self* the coach believes the player and the team are capable of achieving. It is an inspiring vision, seen in its early stages only by the coach. Invariably, it is more than the players believe they are capable of achieving. Just as invariably, achieving the vision will take more effort and hard work than the team is initially willing to put forth.

Resistance to the new vision and the challenge of achieving it is inevitable. You don't attract followers by promising change. People fear change and resist it. What attracts followers is what lies beyond the change. The promise of something better than the current condition. The vision.

As a coach you are a salesperson; you must sell the team on your vision. You must convince your people that they can be better than they are now. Your cornerstones are the small successes, the first victories—for success does breed success. You remind them of their past victories, as my father did in his letter, and then you use your past victories as a springboard for your next challenge.

As we have seen, the January 4, 1963 letter to the Green Bay players was intended to fortify their self-esteem. But it had a second purpose, a purpose equally as important. The letter was a reconfirmation of the vision of excellence Coach Lombardi had for those players; a vision of world championships, a vision of character, commitment, mental toughness, and tenacity.

And here is the essence of coaching—the vision and the communication of the vision—that clear, precise picture of where the coach wants the team to be six months, a year, five years from now.

You have to have a past history of some success to give yourself status and self confidence. You have to accomplish something before you can believe in yourself.
—Y. A. Tittle

The world stands aside to let anyone pass who knows where he is going.
—David Jordan Starr

> *As I paused to think of something*
>   *that set some men apart;*
> *It seemed to me that goals in life*
>   *must be the place to start.*
> *Imagine playing football*
>   *on an unmarked field of green;*
> *Not a goal line to be sought*
>   *not a goal post to be seen.*
> *It would be an aimless battle*
>   *were nothing to be gained;*
> *Without a thing to strive for*
>   *not a score to be attained.*
> *We must have a purpose in our lives*
>   *for the flame that warms the soul;*
> *Is an everlasting vision*
>   *every man must have his goal.*
>   *—Unknown*

Winners can tell you where they are going, what they plan to do along the way, and who will be sharing the adventure with them.
—Dennis Waitley

Vince Lombardi waited—was forced to wait—until he was 47 years old to become a head football coach, while other, younger men were hired. He spent that time well; rather than fret about lost opportunities, he planned and thought, observed and reflected and learned from each experience. And when he finally became head coach of the Packers, he knew exactly what he wanted for his team, and he knew precisely how he was going to obtain it.

I think in the long run the time I had to wait helped me more than anything else.
—Vincent T. Lombardi

A few years ago I was invited to speak at the annual conference of a large corporation. After my presentation, I had dinner with several of the company's top executives. The topic of conversation was the company's just announced reorganization plan. One of the top executives, let's call him Ed, explained in great detail why he believed the reorganization was going to fail. He gave chapter and verse on the flaws in the plan. Now, I was in no position to judge whether Ed's points were correct or not; for all I knew he was right on the money. But what I remember most from that dinner was a question posed by a vice president. He asked Ed, "How would you recommend reorganizing the company?" There was an awkward silence. Ed was stumped, he had no answer. For all his thought on the shortcomings of the reorganization plan, Ed had failed to form his own vision for his company's future.

Unless you can easily and graphically describe the vision it will be difficult for your team to know what they are expected to do to achieve it, or to recognize the value of pursuing it. During periods of stress and tension the team will lose sight of the vision unless it is clear and explicit. The vision must be moving and inspirational. An inspiring vision unites the team to achieve the desired end result and gives the workplace meaning and purpose so the team can feel good abut its struggle.

The vision must be one people can put into their hearts, not just their wallets. It must appeal to what is important to each individual. Each player must be able to see the pay value, the personal profitability—financial, yes, but emotional and psychological as well—that comes from achieving the vision.

It is critical that the coach and the team look beyond current reality. In most cases we construct our vision, the way we want things to be,

The best leaders, almost without exception at every level, are master users of stories and symbols.

—Tom Peters

Once you agree upon the price you and your family must pay for success, it enables you to ignore the minor hurts, the opponents' pressure, and the temporary failures.

—Vincent T. Lombardi

from the way things are. Our vision for the future is oftentimes confined by the circumstances in which we currently find ourselves. This won't do for a team like the 1959 Packers, coming off a season of 1 win, 1 tie, 10 losses, a whirlpool of frustration that, unchecked, will draw more athletes and coaches into the cycle of failure.

A vision that moves and inspires to world championships must be created without reference to the past, without reference to what seems possible at the moment. Otherwise we are prone to limit the vision to what appears to be realistic, and where is the drive and energy and inspiration in that?

The coach must then sell the team on the vision.

Ultimately, visions get translated into sales and profit growth and return on investment, but the numbers come after the vision. In the old-style companies, the numbers are the vision.
—John Naisbitt and
   Patricia Aburdene

I am not going before that ball club without being able to exude assurance.
—Vincent T.
   Lombardi

The Winning Coach

Certainly a leader needs a clear vision of the organization and where it is going, but a vision is of little value unless it is shared in a way to generate enthusiasm and commitment. Leadership and communication are inseparable.

—Claude I. Taylor

Communication

Clearly there is no single way to be a successful team builder. As proof, we have only to play a word association game. Put one adjective next to the names of these team builders. Vince Lombardi, Red Auerbach, Don Shula, Bill Walsh, Pat Riley, Lee Iaccoca, Woody Hayes, Golda Meir, Margaret Thatcher, Abe Lincoln, Franklin Delano Roosevelt, Norman Schwartzkopf, Dwight Eisenhower, Mary Kay Ash, Winston Churchill, Joe Paterno, Bobby Knight, Bill Parcells, and Jack Welch.

You would have used the words charismatic, demanding, tough, cool, intense, explosive, statesmanlike, unshakable. Different people bring different styles to coaching. In my opinion, however, these leaders and others of their caliber share certain qualities in common:

- An inspiring vision and the communication

skills to transmit the vision to their people
- The communication skills to build a consensus; to get people to work together to achieve the vision
- The communication skills to engender enthusiasm within their team to achieve the vision
- Finally, a willingness to lead

Burt Nanus, author of *Visionary Leadership*, described these qualities this way:

"Effective leaders have agendas; they are results oriented. They adopt challenging new visions of what is both possible and desirable and communicate their visions and persuade others to become so committed to these new directions that they are eager to lend their resources and energies to make them happen."

Without doubt, communication skills rank high on the list of qualities a successful leader should possess. Good coaches understand three things about communication:

1. Good ideas don't sell themselves.
2. *Everything* you do as a coach is a form of communication. People never take their eyes off of you.
3. It's not so much what you say, it's *how* you say it, that matters.

It's important that people know what you stand for. It's equally important that they know what you won't stand for.

—Mary Waldrop

Albert Mehrebian, years ago, did a landmark study on the factors that influence face-to-face communication. Mehrebian determined that **7** percent of the impact in face-to-face communication was verbal—the words that are said. Vocal impact accounted for **38** percent—how the words were said, the inflection and the emphasis we place on the words. Finally, Mehrebian found that fully **55** percent of the impact was nonverbal—in other words, body language!

As a professional speaker, I'm well aware that

what I say is less important than *how* I say it—and my body language carries great impact. I may not like it, but that's how it is.

As a coach, you are bound by these same truths. You not only need to walk your talk, you must talk your talk. Your people need to see your face, hear your voice, and witness your body language. It is essential that your talk reflect confidence, assuredness, and genuine enthusiasm. Your people must believe *you* believe what you're saying. If you don't, they can tell immediately.

In any organization communication starts at the top and filters down. As a coach and leader you must tell your team what you know, when you know it. You must give your people all the information they need to do their job. Where is this organization going, and where are we in relation to where we're going? Peter Drucker calls this "Organizational Clarity." If there's some unsettling news in all of this, if it's not all peaches and cream, tell your people. They can handle it, and they will appreciate your being up front and honest with them.

A large western utility hired a consultant who brought his own vocabulary. Before long the utility was completely "jargonized"—to its detriment. In converting the utility's managers to his vocabulary, the consultant alienated people; they had difficulty understanding one another. Said one employee, "I have to get out my dictionary just to understand my manager." The message is clear. If you want to communicate with your people, speak *their* language.

Don't think for a minute that you've successfully communicated with your people because you've held a meeting or written a memo. Communication doesn't take place unless and until your people:

- Hear or see what you have to say
- Understand it

The strength of the group is in the strength of the leader. Many mornings when I am worried or depressed, I have to give myself a pep talk, because I am not going before that ball club without being able to exude assurance. I must be the first believer, because there is no way you can hoodwink the players.

—Vincent T. Lombardi

Action and inaction are perhaps stronger forms of communication than words.

—Monte Hayman

I never tell a football team anything that I don't absolutely believe myself. I always tell them the truth. I can't even try to deceive them, because they'd know. I'd know, so they'd know.

—Vincent T. Lombardi

- Believe it
- Believe you mean it
- Remember it
- Internalize it
- And begin to use it themselves

The greatest problem with communication is the illusion that it's been completed.
—George Bernard Shaw

Then perhaps you can assume you've communicated with your people. At the outset, only you have the information. Therefore, it's your responsibility to see to it that your people understand your message.

Honda of North America uses what they call "the rule of nine" when communicating with one another: *If you want someone to hear you, repeat the message nine times.* Repetition is the key for successfully communicating with your team.

It's not what you say. It's what they hear.
—sign in an office

Communicating your commitment to the inspiring vision is the absolute number one priority for you as a coach. One speech won't do it. One memo won't do it. It takes repetition and constant reinforcement. You must say it and do it over and over and over with enthusiasm and intensity. Don't have enough time? Too busy with other duties? Hire someone to do those other things!

To win, the team must somehow get the feeling that there is a dedication coming from the top and it must be worth something.
—Vincent T. Lombardi

One of the most important qualities of a successful coach is your willingness to communicate. Not the *ability* to communicate, but the *willingness* to communicate. The willingness to haul yourself out of your office to talk with your people is so vital because today's workforce, more than any other previous generation of workers, is demanding that you do so.

People are flooded with all sorts of information today—CNN, C-Span, Prodigy, Compuserve, talk radio, *USA Today,* other newspapers, magazines, and even computer networks. They have come to expect the same flow of information at work. When they don't get timely, up-to-date information in the workplace, the vacuum is only too apparent. And your people will fill the vacuum with the thing you don't want—rumor based on misinformation.

Survey after survey has shown that the farther you move down through a business organization, the less confidence there is that the people at the top can lead and show the way. As a coach, you must be visible and approachable. You have to be "out there." You must tell the truth, though it may be painful, and you must be understanding and compassionate, even though there's nothing you can do about an employee's particular problem at the moment. A coach who is visible, honest, and understanding encourages his people to communicate back.

People who feel they can speak openly—who feel they can say something without having their leader jump down their throats—will express their ideas freely. But if people don't see you, what are they going to conclude? You don't care! And if you don't care, why should they?

If you are not with your people, talking and listening, then you don't know what's going on in your organization. You will have deprived yourself of the free flow of ideas that can quickly uncover potential problems—problems that can be solved while they are small. Harvey Mackay, in his book *Swim with the Sharks Without Being Eaten Alive* says the speed with which you get bad news is a reliable gauge of what kind of leader you are. No one wants to be the bearer of bad tidings, especially if the bearer is likely to be resented. You must be approachable, so that your people's inclination to be quiet about problems can be overcome.

In a team setting, however, the most important aspect of communication is from the bottom up. It's axiomatic—*people closest to the job know best how to do it.*

Have you ever wondered why we have one mouth and two ears? It's because as coaches and

Don't hide your strategy under a bushel. Communicate it throughout your company. Make it all pervasive and let it set a tone and a character to your organization. It's better today to disclose too much than too little.

—Joel E. Ross and Michael J. Kami

The crowd will follow a leader who marches twenty steps in advance; but if he is a thousand steps in front of them, they do not see and do not follow him.

—George Brandes

A man to be a hero must not content himself with heroic virtues and anonymous action. He must talk and explain as he acts— drama.

—William Allen White

You have to set the tone and pace, define objectives and strategies, demonstrate through personal example what you expect from others.

—Stanley Gault

leaders we should be listening a whole lot more than we should be talking. You have a variety of assets in your business—brick and mortar, inventory and capital equipment, and if you're lucky, some cash. But day in day out, in good times and bad, your most important asset is your people.

To the degree that you have problems *today:* The only people who can help you solve those problems *today* are the people who are working for you *today.* Don't waste your most valuable asset. Listen, listen, listen.

A woman came to the Roman emperor Hadrian with a request. He brushed her off because he was busy and had no time for the woman. "Cease then to be emperor," she cried. Hadrian accepted the rebuke and listened to the woman.

And it's not enough to merely listen. Good coaches listen skillfully. Abraham Zaleznik, in his book *The Managerial Mystique,* lays out the qualities of a good listener:

1. Take an active interest in the other person.

2. Suspend judgment until all the facts are known.

3. Listen with a "third ear" to discover what the person wants but doesn't or can't say.

When my father joined the New York Giants as an assistant coach in 1954, he brought a reputation of having been an outstanding high school and college coach, but he was new to pro football. He might have taken the attitude "I'm the coach, you do it my way." Instead, he chose to ask the players, those closest to the job, for help.

During his first training camp, after the evening meeting, my father would wander up to the players' dorm and talk strategy and kick around how a certain play could be run better. Veteran players like Frank Gifford, Charlie

When you hire a pair of hands you get a head for free. Use it.
—Unknown

Most of the successful people I've known are the ones who do more listening than talking. If you choose your company carefully, it's worth listening to what they have to say. You don't have to blow out the other fellow's light to let your own shine.
—Bernard Baruch

Conerly, and Kyle Rote, once they grasped that my father was sincere in asking for their help, opened up and shared their expertise. Despite his reputation for being a martinet, Vince Lombardi was a coach who listened to his players. With Jim Lee Howell as coach and Vince Lombardi and Tom Landry among his assistants the Giants went from being a very average team in 1954 to winning the NFL Championship in 1956.

I make progress by having around me people who are smarter than I am—and listening to them. And I assume that everyone is smarter about something than I am.
—Henry J. Kaiser

Positive Pygmalion

World's greatest management principle: You can work miracles by having faith in others. To get the best out of people, choose to think and believe the best about them.

—Anonymous

Tvemenedous Example!

Pygmalion was a king, a hero of Greek mythology. He was also a sculptor of such rare talent that when he envisioned a picture of a beautiful woman, he was able to create an ivory statue in her lovely image. Moreover, the statue turned out to be so lifelike that Pygmalion fell in love with it. And his love for the statue was so strong and powerful—so the story goes—that the goddess of love, Aphrodite, turned the statue into a real woman of flesh and blood.

The Pygmalion story can be turned to good use in our discussion of leadership and coaching. Pygmalion and his wonderful creation provide us with examples of two important elements in coaching: expectation and transformation. If you, in your position of authority as a coach, have a picture for your team, and if you persistently treat your team in accordance with your picture, they eventually will *get the picture!* Your team will then act and perform as you see them and as you treat them.

It is vitally important for you as a coach to understand how powerful you are. How you see

Treat people as if they were what they ought to be, and you help them to become what they are capable of being.

—Goethe

A new idea is delicate. It can be killed by a sneer or a yawn; it can be stabbed to death by a quip and worried to death by a frown on the right man's brow.
—Charles Browner

your people and how you treat them determines what you get from your people.

Pause with me here for a little self-examination. Ask yourself: *"How do I see my people? What are my expectations for them?"* Your answers are critical to your success. This is no time for platitudes about the dignity and worthiness of people. This is a time to be very honest—remember you're having this conversation with yourself. What are your core beliefs about people?

Consider the spectrum of beliefs below: At one end, people are seen as lazy, incompetent and irresponsible. On the other end people are believed to be creative, reliable, and worthy of our trust.

Lazy			Creative
Incompetent	⊢————————⊣		Reliable
Irresponsible			Trustworthy

An automobile goes nowhere efficiently unless it has a quick, hot spark to ignite things, to set the cogs in the machine in motion. So I try to make every player on my team feel he's the spark keeping our machine in motion. On him depends our success.
—Knute Rockne

Where do your beliefs fall along this spectrum? Do you believe you must be ever vigilant in supervising people, constantly "on" them so they don't slack off? Or do you view most people as self-starters, full of potential and energy, needing only guidance?

Computer software companies have a reputation for giving their employees a lot of latitude, of guiding them with a loose rein. In explanation, we are told that these people are "creative" types who wouldn't function well under close supervision and control, self-starters who need only loose direction.

I wonder if another explanation might be closer to the truth. Is it not possible that this successful creativity is the result of people being creative *because* they're left alone to do their work and are treated as reliable self-starters? Why not assume the creative energy seen in this class of workers can be tapped in everyone, if only we have the courage and the faith to trust our people to be reliable and responsible?

Don't be defensive about this. Our world view, our core beliefs are mostly the result of our conditioning and upbringing, so there's no cause for blame or guilt. Until recently, conventional wisdom tended to see people as irresponsible and incompetent. Not surprisingly, the organizational structures we adopted reflected this world view. And what was this structure? From the top down, a definite hierarchy of control, power assigned by virtue of title and position. The message couldn't have been clearer if we put a big sign over the employee entrance: *If we don't have somebody at the top telling you what to do, we know you'll screw up!*

This type of top-down organizational structure attracted universal sanction as America emerged from World War II. Since this was the type of structure that beat the Germans and the Japanese, how could it not succeed in the workplace? In actuality, this kind of thinking—"People will screw up if somebody at the top isn't telling them what to do"—existed long before World War II. This mindset gave us the father as the head of the family, the divine right of kings, and generals in the army, long before World War II. And that's why most business organizations have a President and CEO.

This organizational structure gives you and me, as business people, the two things we value the most—stability and predictability.

Recently, many of us have begun to rethink our view of people. Gradually, we're beginning to see people as competent and creative, and our organizational structures have begun to reflect this fundamental and important shift. We're reorganizing and reengineering and empowering our people—and asking them to do a whole lot more with a whole lot less. Partly this has been a result of the success of the Japanese, partly it's

Security is mostly a superstition. It does not exist in nature, nor do the children of men as a whole experience it. Avoiding danger is no safer than outright exposure. Life is either a daring adventure or nothing.
—Helen Keller

We live in a world of change, yet we act on the basis of continuity.
—Leon Martel

due to the fact that we've moved away from assembly-line work and more toward value-added and knowledge-based work. Mainly it's a matter of survival—either we change, or we perish.

Things are moving too fast in today's world for conventional approaches. The very advances in technology we're so proud of are overwhelming us with information, to the point that the inherently ponderous nature of a top-down organization is a luxury we can no longer afford. It's too slow, too cumbersome, too inefficient.

Consider: Of the top 25 companies listed on the Fortune 500 list in 1955, only 14 remain on the list today. Six have dropped out of the top 25—two of the six are not even among the top 100—and five have ceased to exist. Additionally, 143 companies that were on the Fortune 500 list *five years ago* are no longer there!

In the past, life was simpler—you could dominate your industry for years because of the sheer quality of your product. And if, in time, a rival would begin to compete with you on quality, you could respond with lower prices or improved service, and you would be the industry leader once again. Today, your domination may be complete, but by tomorrow competitors are popping up worldwide, competing with you on quality, price, and service.

You have only to look at Sears, IBM and General Motors to see the fate of companies that try to predict their future by looking to their past. These were top-down organizations that placed a tremendous premium on stability and predictability, and forgot that no one can predict the future. Moreover, no one can hold stable the present and make it captive to the future.

Perhaps you see these hard truths as applying to someone else. Perhaps you are saying, yes, I read the financial pages and, yes, I'm aware of the problems that IBM, Sears, and General

Businessmen tend to grow old early. They are committed to security and stability. They won't rock the boat and won't gamble; denying the future for a nearsighted present. They forget what made them successful in the first place.
—Peter Goldmark

Motors are experiencing. But they are big and I am small, you say. What relevance can their mistakes have for me?

That's a fair comment, but let's remember one thing: Companies don't fail, people fail. As Peter Drucker says: *In a business sense, every failure is the failure of a manager.* People and managers are the same whether they're sitting in the Sears Tower in Chicago, Detroit, IBM's headquarters in suburban New York City, or in a chair reading this book.

Sears had a blind spot—it didn't see K Mart and Wal-Mart as its competition because there was nothing in its history that predicted this type of competitor. Indeed, in a 1980s position paper compiled by Sears on its competition, the author never mentioned Wal-Mart!

GM, grown fat and sassy from the profits on the big cars it made synonymous with Detroit, couldn't bring itself to believe that Americans would drive small cars. There was nothing in the company's rearview mirror that would have told it so. Then Japan attacked with Toyotas and Nissans, and the lesson was driven home.

Nor was IBM—Big Blue, the favorite of a generation of investors—immune to the sin of looking in the wrong direction. So successful with its profitable mainframe computers, IBM failed to see that new technology—ironically much of it IBM's own—had created a burgeoning new industry built around personal computers and work stations. IBM had the technology for PCs, and they sat on it, fearing PCs would cut into their profits on mainframes!

Look at your organization as it exists right now:

- Is your team built on a top-down framework?
- Is there a definite hierarchy of control?
- Do you hold your power by virtue of your title?

Business more than any other occupation is a continual dealing with the future, it is continual calculation, an instinctive exercise in foresight.

—Henry R. Luce

The graveyards are full of indispensable men.

—Charles DeGaulle

- Are your people there just to follow your orders?
- Must everyone look to you for the answers?
- Are you suspicious of ideas that don't originate with you?
- Is your first reaction to an idea from someone else to turn it down?
- Do you constantly need to be in control?

We've got to make sure we don't create organizations with a CEO at the top, a computer in the middle, and a lot of workers at the bottom.

—Robert T. Tomako

Answer yes to many of these questions and chances are you're experiencing some problems. If you see the people who work for you as losers, as disposable and replaceable, they will reflect your vision as faithfully as any mirror. If you see your people as "less than," if you treat your people as "less than," they will act and perform as "less than." You will then see your self-fulfilling prophecies come true. You will catch yourself saying "I knew he couldn't do that." "I knew she couldn't pull that off; I've been saying that, I've been thinking that all along." And you will be right—although you wouldn't have been if your expectations for your people had been different at the outset.

Each season in almost every professional sport, we see players who haven't played to their potential traded to another team and have an outstanding season. The players' new success is attributed to a "change of scenery." Oftentimes this "change of scenery" has nothing to do with geography. Rather, the player responds to the direction of a new coaching staff, one without preconceived ideas about his ability and thus willing to give the player time to show his true ability. In sports and business, lack of production is often more the result of poor direction than poor execution.

If your company's organizational chart reads from the top down, it's likely you are slow to react to change, you are inefficient, and you are out of touch with your customers. And I'll make two more predictions: employee morale is low, and turnover is high.

All this affects your business internally, but there's a serious external cost to a top-down style of organization, too. Have you considered the possibility that the Golden Rule may be in play within your organization? That your people are treating your customers in a manner similar to the way they are being treated? If the way you control and supervise your people sends them a message that they are not valued, that they lack the intelligence to do their job, then what kind of message do you suppose your employees are sending your customers? Pygmalion!

Is quality lagging in your department, despite constant emphasis and reminders? Is it possible that because of your core beliefs, you have failed to distinguish between the things you produce and the people you lead? With things you can afford to be coldly efficient, but to be effective with people, you must build relationships. Your opinion of your people and your expectations for them go to the very heart of your effectiveness with your people. Do you understand that the quality of your products and the quality of your service flow directly from the quality of your team?

"Pygmalion coaches" understand that for their organization to be brought to life, for the mission to succeed, everyone must be involved, not just the small core of managers at the top. Pygmalion coaches believe people have dignity and that most everyone will accept responsibility and take accountability. The core belief of successful coaches is that people come to work eager to do a good job, and these coaches understand that if workers are afforded trust and respect, they will respond in a positive, constructive fashion. They will respond quickly to change, and will exhibit a spirit of cooperation that allows the organi-

If you don't keep your employees happy, they won't keep the customers happy.
—Anonymous

There is no reward for finding fault.
—Arnold Glascow

Quality products and services evolve from work environments.
—Sam L. Moore

Quality goes up when management has high expectations for their staff.
—Unknown

We treat people like royalty. If you honor and serve people who work for you, they will honor and serve you.
—Mary Kay Ash

Praise does wonders for the sense of hearing.
—Unknown

zation to attack new challenges with a can-do attitude.

Good coaches have a positive Pygmalion streak in them. Weak coaches, on the other hand, wait for the players to come along and make them winners. They sit around saying in effect, "Well, what do you expect? Nobody could win with these losers, these jerks they keep sending me." But the good coaches say, "It doesn't matter who we've got! We're going to win anyway, because I'm such a good coach, I'm such a good teacher, I'll transform these people into champions."

Ask yourself: "How do I see my people, my team? Is it possible that the picture I hold for my people, and the way I treat them, influences their habits, their attitudes, their beliefs, and ultimately their performance?"

The military has long been regarded as a classic example of a top-down organization, and most observers feel that its willingness to see the enlisted ranks as capable and competent is a recent development. Yet the principle of investing trust to achieve results has been a part of military doctrine for a very long time. Here is what Major General John Schofield said in 1879:

> "The discipline which makes soldiers of a free country reliable in battle is not to be gained by harsh or tyrannical treatment. On the contrary, such treatment is far more likely to destroy than make an army. It is possible to impart instructions and give commands in such a manner and such a tone of voice to inspire in the soldier no feeling but an intense desire to obey, while the opposite manner and tone of voice cannot fail to excite strong resentment and a desire to disobey. The one mode or the other of dealing with subordinates springs from a corresponding spirit in the breast of the commander. He who feels the respect

Approval is a great motivator. I try to follow any criticism, whenever possible, with a pat on the back, realizing I cannot antagonize and influence at the same time.
—John Wooden

Flatter me, and I may not believe you. Criticize me, and I may not like you. Ignore me, and I may not forgive you. Encourage me, and I will not forget you.
—William Arthur Ward

Trust men and they will be true to you; treat them greatly and they will show themselves to be great.
—Ralph Waldo Emerson

which is due to others cannot fail to inspire in them a regard for himself, while he who feels, and have manifested disrespect toward others, especially his inferiors, cannot fail to inspire hatred against himself."

Mental Locks

Those who say it cannot be done should get out of the way of those who are doing it.

—Anonymous

When I was much younger, I once read that only five percent of the people in a given profession truly aim for excellence in their work. At the time I thought the statement too harsh. Now, decades later, I consider the estimate to be too generous.

Yet even more amazing are the studies showing that we use only eight to ten percent of our total brain power! Some recent research indicates that most of us fall short of even this discouraging number—most of us use no more than three, two, or one percent of our resources. This is important for you as a coach, for it suggests possibilities of dramatic improvement in your workplace. Consider: if you had 100 people working with you and you could find a way to get 1 percent more productivity from each of them. That would be a gain of a hundredfold! Think of the difference that would make for you and your organization.

Why do 95 percent of us settle for so little in our aspirations and our accomplishments? One reason is that not only are we Pygmalion to the people around us, we are Pygmalion to ourselves. We hand beliefs *about* ourselves *to* ourselves all the time. So the 64 dollar question obviously becomes: what beliefs about myself am I handing to myself? When I say, "This is

One person with belief is equal to a force of ninety-nine who have only interests.
   —John Stuart Mill

Speed is useful only if you're running in the right direction.
   —Joel A. Barker

the kind of person I am," "This is the way things happen for me," am I getting a true answer?

Our thoughts and our beliefs often work to limit and confine us. To coach people to use more of their potential and attain higher levels of performance, we must understand that people don't act in accordance with what may be objectively true. Rather, people act in accordance with the truth as they *perceive* it, the truth as they *believe it to be*. So it is critical that we find answers to some very difficult questions— "Where's the truth?" What do I believe?"

Try this simple exercise. Without looking at your watch take it off your wrist and put it out of sight. Now get a pen and paper. Draw a picture of your watch from memory. Make your picture as detailed as possible—size and shape, color of the face, style of the numbers and the brand name or logo. Does your watch have a second hand? Take a few minutes to complete your drawing, making it as accurate as possible. Now, put your watch back on your wrist. Take a good look. How does your drawing from memory correspond to reality?

Don't be surprised if your drawing differs from your watch in important aspects. How do we explain that despite the fact we look at our watch many times during the day, we miss things? Well, when you look at your watch what do you do? You check to see the time. Over a period of time, as you "lock-on" to the time, you "lock-out" the details of your watch. Over a period of time with this lock-on, lock-out process you build a blind spot to the details of the face of your watch. Looking right at it, you don't see it.

We have blind spots in many different areas of our lives. The interesting thing is that we don't know we have these blind spots. Roger Von Oech calls these blind spots "mental locks." In his book *A Whack On The Side Of The Head*, Von Oech says that sometimes nothing short of a "whack on the side of the head" can dislodge the assumptions that keep us locked-on and locked-out.

You can undoubtedly find examples of these mental locks in your background; so can I. Often during my working career my wife would tell me that I had difficulty with women in the workplace. I would insist this was not the case. The truth was, being in professional football much of my adult life, I had no way of knowing—since there are very few women in pro football.

When I took over the USFL team in Michigan it became immediately apparent that the sharpest person in the organization was the comptroller. *She* had every answer, wasn't afraid to speak up, and had no difficulty making decisions. When people would ask me how the new job was progressing, the first thing I would say was "The best person in the organization is a woman!"

Why was this such a revelation to me? My wife was right, I did have a challenge with women in the workplace and I didn't even know it; I had a blind spot, a mental lock. For me it was Von Oech's whack on the side of the head.

The following year the Michigan team merged with the Oakland team. And surprise! The sharpest, most aggressive person in Oakland was a woman. This time it wasn't such a revelation.

The daughters of lions are lions, too.

—Swahili Proverb

This idea of blind spots, or "mental locks," can be useful to you as a coach. When your people come to you and say, "I don't get it, I don't understand this," or you hear yourself say, "I don't see how we're ever going to get this done," be assured both you and your people are working with mental locks that are handicapping your team.

1889 — Authorities wanted to close the Patent Office, thinking nothing else could possibly be invented.

1939 — Military people concluded, "The Germans can't possibly break through France's Maginot Line."

1951 — "There is a market for no more than five computers."

1954 — "The four-minute mile can't be broken."

1992 — "George Bush has a lock on reelection."

Having difficulty seeing this? Remember when you put your watch back on your wrist? *What time was it?* Interesting, isn't it? Normally when we look at our watch, we lock-on to what time it is and lock-out the details. But a moment ago, you looked at your watch and, because I reversed the critical information, you locked-on to the details of your watch and locked-out the time. Looking right at it, you didn't see it. Just like that, a blind spot to the time.

Progress for your organization will occur when you challenge the rules and try a different way of doing things. Football would still be running the flying wedge if coaches and players hadn't challenged the rules and started throwing the ball. The two hand set shot would still be winning basketball games if someone hadn't gone against conventional wisdom and put up a jump shot.

As a coach you must constantly ask yourself, "Where am I locked-on? Where are my people locked-on?" Are you locked on to traditional ways of doing things? *"We've always done it this way before"* is a deadly, killer phrase. Organizationally and individually, you can't afford to lock-on to the way you did things last week, last month, or last year. If you insist on doing things the way you did them last month, your competition won't, and they'll go by you as though you were standing still.

Sheldon Kopp, psychotherapist and author,

If you don't keep doing it better . . . Your competition will.

—*Anonymous*

Never will a man penetrate deeper into error than when he is continuing on a road that has led him to great success.

—*Friedreich Von Hayek*

tells a story that illustrates this lock-on, lock-out concept:

> *A man finds himself in a dark, barren cell with the only source of light a small barred window. He sees the window as his only source of hope, and strains toward the window, clinging to the bars. So intent is the prisoner on keeping the light of the window in sight—so locked-on is he to the conviction that only the window can offer him release— that it never enters his mind to let go and explore the rest of his cell. If he could bring himself to do so, he would discover that the door at the far end of the cell is unlocked and he is free to leave—but only if he will let go.*

Perhaps you're locked-on to something out of emotional attachment, perhaps a technique you were first exposed to when you got into your particular line of work. "That's it, I've got it, don't confuse me with the facts." In the process of holding to the tried and true, are you locking-out easier, more productive ways of doing things?

Are you locked-on to a first impression, an entry level picture for someone? Perhaps an associate, an employee, a customer? And right before your eyes, these people are growing and changing, but you can't see it because you're so locked-on to that first impression, that entry level picture.

Let me tell you a story about the importance of being willing to reevaluate first impressions. In 1961 the Packers' first round draft choice was an All-American out of Michigan State by the name of Herb Adderley, a great athlete with size and speed. My father envisioned Adderley as a running back, his college position, but he didn't quite fit in. My father moved him to the flanker position. There, Adderley seemed more at home, but still something was missing; he would look great in practice but failed to produce in the games.

If you think there is only one right answer, then you'll stop looking as soon as you find one.
—Roger Von Oech

Challenge conventional wisdom, especially cause and effect relations that have been considered axiomatic.
—Tom Peters

It's amazing what ordinary people can do if they set out without preconceived notions.
—Charles Kettering

Minds that don't change are like clams that don't open.
—Ursula Le Guin

If you only look at what is, you might never attain what could be.

—Unknown

It was halfway through the season before another player gave my father the key. Adderley didn't want to play offense where he took the blows, said the player, he wanted to play defensive back, where he *delivered* the blows.

My father had been so locked-on to his picture of Adderley as an offensive player that he nearly mishandled him. Today, Herb Adderley is in the Pro Football Hall of Fame, a tribute to his ability and a coach's willingness to "unlock" a first impression.

Examining past beliefs is painful but instructive. Let's go back in time to the 1960s and recall what we believed to be some enduring truths. Gasoline was cheap; we knew that to be a fact, because oil from the Middle East would always be plentiful. Another was the size of our cars—chrome, tailfins, and all. Surely buyers would continue to prefer size and be willing to pay for it. Still another "truth" of that period was that anything made in Japan was cheap, second-rate, and of poor quality.

Do you suppose things might be a little different in Detroit today if automobile people in the 1960s weren't so locked-on to cheap gas, big cars, and contempt for items "made in Japan"?

Stepping forward to the 1970s, diversification was the watchword for business. Sears, already dominating the retail business it knew best, branched out into real estate, the brokerage and insurance business, and other ventures.

Sears was so locked-on to its diversification program that it developed a blind spot to the rapid changes taking place in the retail business, fostered primarily by Wal-Mart. The result is clear today. Sears, once the colossus of the retail industry, is scrambling to rediscover its identity—trying, in the process, to divest itself of everything not related to its core business of retailing. Today Wal-Mart is the big company and Sears, trying harder as befits a company that's no longer No. 1, is developing some quick and agile moves of its own.

Finally, we can look at IBM, an organization with a strong corporate belief in "this is how we do things around here." IBM based its success on mainframe computers and super salespeople who handled its own distribution system. If you wanted to buy an IBM computer you had to deal with an IBM salesperson, who was knowledgeable, polite, and not at all interested in negotiating price.

Along came the PC and computer stores that gave you a wide range of choices. You could shop equipment and price, pay for your computer, and take it home with you. IBM was so locked-on to its formula for success that it failed to react to the changes in the marketplace fostered by fast and nimble team-oriented companies—companies that were able to navigate around the mental locks that then existed in the computer industry.

Joel Arthur Barker, who has done pioneering work on paradigms, tells this story:

> *A young man, whose passion was driving his classic sports car, was one day happily driving in the mountains, up and down the hills, around the corners, wind blowing in his face. But as he came around a corner, there was a car in his lane! He swerved one direction, the other car swerved the same way. He swerved the other way, and the other car matched him! At last a collision was averted, but as the other car flashed past, the other driver, a young woman, yelled, "Pig!" The young man yelled back, "Sow!" Thinking to himself, "Nobody calls me a name and gets away with it." He shifted into the next corner and promptly ran into the biggest pig you ever saw, totaling his beautiful car.*

No corporation gets hit by the future between the eyes. They always get hit in the temple.
—Dick Davis

Most organizations that fall short of their goals do so not because of stupidity or faulty doctrines, but because of internal decay and rigidification. They grow stiff in the joints. They get in a rut. They go to seed.
—John Gardner

When one door closes, another door opens; but we often look so long and so regretfully upon the closed door that we do not see the ones which open for us.
—Alexander Graham Bell

The young man heard the word, but missed the warning. We can smile at this story but the message is important. Are you so locked-on to what you absolutely know to be true that when people shout warnings to you, you can't hear them? Can you see opportunities, or do your mental locks make you miss what's right in front of you?

Years ago, Leon Festinger gave us a concept called Cognitive Dissonance or the "thought conflict" theory. Festinger determined, through his research, that a person can only hold one strong belief or opinion about a single topic at one time. Conversely, he can't hold two conflicting beliefs or opinions about the same thing at the same time. If you are convinced that "This is the way things happen around here," you are certain to react negatively if confronted with an opposite opinion or belief. Moreover, the confrontation will make you uptight and nervous.

It would be like having your finger in a live light socket and whenever you're confronted with an opposite opinion or idea, someone would flip the switch. Each new idea would give you a jolt—*zap*. If you're reading the morning paper, and right there on the front page you're confronted with something that differs with your belief, *zap*—you get a jolt. On the car radio on your way to work there would be another opposing opinion. *Zap*. Then at work, on the phone, in a meeting, during lunch—*zap, zap, zap*. Well, no one wants to go through life with their finger in a light socket.

Everyone hears only what he understands.
—Goethe

If the only tool you have is a hammer, you tend to see every problem as a nail.
—Abraham Maslow

So what do we do? We build blind spots to all these different ideas and opposing opinions. Looking right at them, we don't see them; listening, we don't hear them. We tenaciously lock-on to our own opinions and beliefs and lock-out different and opposing points of view.

With whom do you associate, share coffee and lunch? People who think like you do and come from the same background? How diverse is your workforce? Who do you hire? People in your own image, probably, people with ideas and opinions that mirror your own. So many of us have picked a job applicant by saying, "Hey, she must be smart, she thinks the same way I do."

When you form a task force to solve a problem or put together a team, who do you select? People who have been through the same things as you have. People with whom you are comfortable. Why not, they think like you do!

In ancient times, kings would keep a court jester handy to lampoon and poke holes in the advice of the king's counselors and to ease the tension even monarchs feel. A "jester" might be a valuable addition to your team, to bring a new way of seeing things, a fresh approach to old problems. Someone who is a little irreverent, a little off-beat, might provide you with a little "whack" on the side of the head when you need to solve a problem creatively.

I was once associated with the National Football League Management Council, the collective bargaining agent for pro football owners. In 1982 we were negotiating a collective bargaining agreement with the NFL Players Association. The players' major demand was that 52 percent of the NFL's gross revenue be paid to the players. We rejected this demand without consideration. We didn't want the players as partners, and we didn't want them looking at our books. No way!

In those days, when a player or his agent negotiated a contract they didn't know what other players were being paid, other than summaries, by position. They negotiated blind, so to speak. In 1982 this changed, because the National Labor Relations Board ruled that the NFL had to turn over to the Players Association all player contract information. Ed Garvey, the head of the Players Association, grasped the signi-

Do not make them in your image. Do not even try. My assistants do not look alike, think alike or have the same personalities. And I sure do not want them thinking alike or like I do.

—Bear Bryant

If everyone is thinking alike, then someone isn't thinking.

—George S. Patton

ficance of the NLRB ruling, and told the Management Council that when players knew each other's salary, contract negotiations would change dramatically and salaries would skyrocket. Under the changed circumstances, he said, the union's proposal for a percentage of gross was not unreasonable. His lecture went in one ear and out the other.

We were so locked-on to opposing the concept of percentage of the gross that we locked-out the possibility that Garvey was right. After 1982, NFL salaries escalated rapidly, partly due to the emergence of the United States Football League, but principally because every player and his agent now knew what every other NFL player was earning, and could compare his contract with every other player in the league.

In 1993, the NFL agreed to pay the players 64 percent of gross revenue in salaries, League pensions, and other benefits. If the NFL had accepted the union's demand for a percentage of the gross in 1982, would that percentage be higher in 1993? Of course. Would it be at 64 percent? I doubt it.

You need diverse thinking on your team. Successful coaches encourage and respect different ideas and points of view. If your assistants always agree with you, it's likely you are receiving mediocre advice.

The "truth" as we see it is oftentimes clouded by our blind spots. All of our senses are affected by our mental locks. We can't see past them, and consequently, we see our world in only one way—"our way." The danger for you as a coach is that you take your blind spots, your mental locks, and convert them into a rigid insistence of "this is the way it is." Then a different idea or point of view isn't just different; for you it's wrong, and you dismiss it.

When my father took over the Green Bay Packers, they didn't know how to win. To return

It's great to work with somebody who wants to do something differently.
—Keith Bellows

Diversity, the art of thinking differently, together.
—Malcolm Forbes

It is important not to mistake the edge of the rut for the horizon.
—Anonymous

to the wristwatch analogy, they didn't know what time it was. They had a blind spot to their ability to be winners. It took a strong Pygmalion like my father—someone with high self-esteem, a great sense of resiliency, and the strength of conviction to impose his vision of victory on a group of players inured to defeat—to go into that situation and transform those players into champions. He believed in them so intensely that they began to believe in themselves. He changed their belief system and he redefined their definition of "This is the kind of player I am." Because then, and only then, could he tell them what time it was and show them the new "truth" about their talent and ability. Thirteen of the players who suffered through that 1-10-1 season in Green Bay the year before my father got there went on to be All-Pro.

Just like those players, we're limited by our mental locks. Because of our preconceived way of seeing things, because of our habitual way of doing things, our blind spots cause us to see what we expect to see, ignore what we don't expect to see, hear what we expect to hear, and think the way we expect to think.

One thing we know to be "true" is that marathon runners somewhere after 20 miles hit the "wall." Their bodies experience oxygen debt and they really begin to struggle. We know that marathon runners must train their bodies to persevere through the "wall." Yet the Tarahumara Indians, natives of northwestern Mexico, think nothing of running 70 miles at a crack, as part of a festival. Clearly, the "truth" for the Tarahumara Indians is not the "truth" for the rest of us.

Mental locks are responsible for a whole host of reasons not to change, or even try:

- We've always done it that way before
- We can't do that, it's against policy

Minds are like para-chutes. They only func-tion when they are open.

—Sir James Dewar

- We tried that before, it won't work
- It will take ten years to do that, and besides they'll never let us
- I'm too young
- I'm too old
- I don't have the right training or education
- I'm not the right sex

Good coaches have fewer blind spots than most people. Good coaches are analytical and they are skeptical. They understand that in a given situation their mental locks may be getting in the way of their view of the situation. Therefore, they constantly ask themselves " Where am I locked-on?" and "What am I missing?" Good coaches understand that to grow, to change, to do more, it's not a matter of working harder. (You're already doing that, aren't you?) It's a matter of thinking and working a *little differently*.

So the next time you have some difficulty getting your team to go along with you, the next time your people have difficulty seeing things your way, you might be tempted to say, "These losers, what's the matter with them anyway? Why don't these people see this situation the same way I do? Why won't they accept responsibility or take accountability?"

Resist this temptation! Instead, go back to your office and figure out a better way to show your people. Your people aren't purposely dragging their feet, and they're not avoiding responsibility just to be contrary. They have a different filter system than you do. They've been through a different conditioning process than you have.

They don't know what time it is! They have their own mental locks! And it's up to you as their coach to broaden their range of vision. Because these people—your associates, the people who work for you, your customers—are smart enough if you're good enough to show them the "truth."

There's a misconception about teamwork. Team-work is the ability to have different thoughts about things; it's the ability to argue and stand up and say loud and strong what you feel. But in the end, it's also the ability to adjust to what is best for the team.

—Tom Landry

Motivation and Inspiration

*No leader, however great can long continue
unless he wins the battles . . . I believe it is
essential to understand that the battles are won
primarily in the hearts of men. Men respond to
leadership in a most remarkable way and once
you have won his heart, he will follow you anywhere. Leadership is based on a spiritual quality;
the power to inspire, the power to inspire others
to follow.*

—Vincent T. Lombardi

Would you agree that we've all been exposed
to the same information, more or less, with respect
to what it takes to win? To achieve? To excel?
Would you further agree that if we could develop
this raw material of achievement, this common
knowledge, we could accomplish more, both
individually and organizationally?

Then how to explain why some of us do
achieve, and some do not; why some organizations flourish, and some do not? Why is it that
some of us soar, some of us flame on and
crash—and most inexplicably, some of us fail to
move at all? What distinguishes the successful
coaches from the others? What separates the
winning teams from the also-rans? We all want to
achieve and win, so why don't more of us do it?

The answer, to a great degree, lies in *motivation,* a word often used as a shorthand explanation
for success. "They won, because they were
motivated." "She was motivated to get that
promotion." What, precisely is motivation? Add
a couple of letters to the word motivation, you get
"motive to act" or "motive to action." So one
definition of motivation would be having a "motive to act."

Picture this: A man is sitting in a campsite,
when a loaded station wagon pulls into the adjoin-
ing campsite. The doors pop open, and out

jump two adults and two youngsters. The second their feet hit the ground, the kids take off, searching for firewood. Mom and dad rush around getting the tent set up, the sleeping bags unrolled, and the dinner organized. The man in the next campsite observes all this activity and says to the father, "Pretty impressive display of teamwork!" The father replies, "When we go camping, we have only one rule. Nobody goes to the bathroom until the campsite is set up." That's motivation—having a motive to act.

Motivating Yourself

The essence of motivation is gestalt. By our very nature, we're always working for order, balance, and harmony. All of us have an idea of the way things are supposed to be for us—"This is the kind of leader I am." "This is the way things happen for my team."

I've got a clear idea of the way my speaking business should operate. So many speeches at a specific fee. Busy fifty weeks a year. I should be able to pick and choose the groups I speak to, with lots of opportunities to speak in Arizona, California, and Hawaii during the winter months. Now, when *what I've got* matches *what I want,* when current reality matches my picture of the way things are supposed to be for me—my business is operating the way I want it to. In other words, when I have balance, order, and harmony, I'm content, and my system provides me with just enough drive and energy to maintain the status quo. I'm motivated enough to keep things going, but I'm not motivated to take on a major challenge. This applies to us individually and organizationally.

Things are different when what I've got *doesn't* match what I want. Now I've got a problem. That's a pretty good shorthand definition of a problem—when what I've got doesn't match what I want. If my business or my career isn't progressing the way I think it should, then I have disorder, disharmony, imbalance. And since I'm someone who is always working for balance, order, and harmony—and now I don't have it—I get tense, I get nervous, and I get uptight.

When I perceive I have a problem, I get uncomfortable, as everybody does. This feeling of discomfort, tension, anxiety, and stress can be—*can* be—the drive and energy we call motivation.

I have an idea of how my lawn should look—cut just so, neat and trim. Most evenings in the summer, when I look at my lawn, what I've got matches what I want. The grass looks okay, no problem! I go into the house and get a cold drink. But every seventh day or so, I look at my lawn and it doesn't look right, too long and a little rough around the edges. I've got a problem; what I've got doesn't match what I want. I don't go into the house for a drink, I go into the garage and get the lawn mower. That's motivation!

This feeling of discomfort we all get when we have a problem, this vague feeling of tension, anxiety, and stress we feel when we perceive what we've got doesn't match what we want, can be—*can* be—the drive and energy we call motivation, *if*.

If individually and collectively, we know what we want.

If what we *want* is stronger than what we've *got*.

If our vision—our mission—is clear, precise and vivid.

If we are committed to what we want.

Then when we get uptight, nervous, and tense because we perceive we have a problem, we will convert this tension, this discomfort, into the

Obstacles are things a person sees when he takes his eyes off his goals.
—E. Joseph Cossman

Once you learn to quit, it becomes a habit.
—Vincent T. Lombardi

drive and energy we call motivation to go after what we want.

But what if what we've got is stronger than what we want—if we're going after what we want at about 90 percent? If our goals are nebulous and shaky and nothing more than a good idea? If our team lacks commitment, then when a problem appears—they always do—we get anxious, tense, and uncomfortable? Now, our first thought will not be to pursue the goal. No, our first thought will be, "This tension, this stress, this anxiety, how do I avoid this, how do I get out of this, how do I get back to where I'm comfortable?" At this point many people quit and compromise on what they want. This is why more of us don't grow or change, and why so many teams have such difficulty getting to the next level of performance.

Some people don't set goals, and justify it as a matter of principle—"I don't believe in this goal setting stuff." If that sounds like you, understand one thing. Without goals, dreams, a vision—today will look the same as yesterday and tomorrow will look the same as today.

We need to understand something else here. Human beings are teleological—striving for purpose—it's our very nature to work toward goals. We're meant to be in motion, going after something. If we don't have goals of our own, goals that are vivid, clear, and precise, goals to which we are committed, then we will adopt someone else's goals to pursue. Our goals will then be what our parents want for us, what we saw on television last night, what we read in the latest business journal. I can't imagine anything worse than to be out there, hustling, striving, working, a little uptight, nervous, tense, not for my goals and dreams, but somebody else's.

Some of us do want to grow and accomplish things; we set goals, but we really don't commit to them. We go after our goals at about 80 or 90 percent, holding back just enough to provide a graceful retreat, should one become necessary. So when a problem arises, we want to bail out, to avoid the tension and discomfort.

One way we reduce this tension is to move what we want closer and closer to what we've got—in other words, by compromising on what we want. When we compromise on our goals, it's important to recognize the price we pay. First, we don't go after a compromised goal with anywhere near the drive and energy we use to go after what we initially want. Second, your first compromise invites a second; you get in the habit of compromising. Your system gets a pretty good idea of what your threshold for pain, tension, and anxiety is. It becomes easier to quit, to sit when you should be standing, to walk when you should be running, to move slower and slower.

Some people do want to grow and change, so they set goals and commit to them—their goals are clear and precise—but they never look at current reality. "How are things going?" people ask. "Peachy, dandy, couldn't be better"—when of course they aren't. It's essential that you look at current reality, for that's how you create the tension, the discomfort that—if your goals are strong enough and clear enough—you will convert to the drive and energy we call motivation, to go after what you want. Looking at current reality isn't negative, as long as you understand that current reality is only temporary.

I have a goal to weigh 170 pounds. I can't get there! About the best I can do is 178 pounds. Now, I'm committed to 170 pounds—170 pounds is very clear and precise to me. I can *see* the scale as I step on it and the needle goes to 170. I know how my clothes will *feel* when I weigh 170: loose and comfortable. I can *hear* the compliments: "Vince, you look good, did you lose a little weight?"

Compromise . . . that's when you give the other guy half of what's rightfully yours.
—Sue Grafton

The more often you semi-try or don't try at all on a golf shot, in anger and frustration, the more you accustom yourself to quitting. And, as with swing flaws, the more often this type of behavior is repeated, the more ingrained it becomes.
—Jack Nicklaus

My problem is that I never look at current reality, I never get on the scale now, today. All I do is stand in front of the mirror, examine my face and midsection and tell myself, "Not bad for my age." But you see, there's no tension or discomfort there! If I'm going to get down to 170 pounds I need to get on the scale every morning and confront the reality reflected on the dial. Because 170 pounds is so vivid and clear to me—I can see it, I can feel it, I can hear it—the scale consistently reading 178 pounds will eventually make me so uncomfortable that I'll be motivated to do the things I need to do to lose weight—eat smarter and exercise more.

Ken Blanchard, the coauthor of *The One Minute Manager,* and a coauthor with Don Shula of *Everyone's A Coach,* says "Feedback is the Breakfast of Champions." Great line! Feedback—where I am in relationship to where I want to go, what I've got in relation to what I want—is indeed the breakfast of champions, and is the principal motivator for both you and your team.

Yes, it stings, and, yes, it hurts when we set a goal and we fall short. You lose the game, you don't make the sale, I don't lose the weight, we miss our fourth quarter goals. You feel like you might throw up. You slink around feeling you have a big red "F" for failure painted on your forehead. You want to crawl into a hole, hide out in the restroom, and skip this morning's meeting. Be clear on this: **that's the price you pay to get into the arena!**

Failure is part and parcel of being successful. The price you pay in setting a goal is the risk of failure. The price for not setting a goal is much higher: stagnation and decay.

The movie *A League of Their Own,* about a women's baseball league formed during World War II, contains a memorable scene. The manager of one of the teams faced the prospect of losing his star player for the championship game, because her husband had returned from overseas and wanted her to quit playing baseball. The manager asked her why she was leaving at such a crucial time, and she said, "It's gotten too hard." "Hard!" the manager exclaims, "Of course it's hard! If it was easy everybody would do it. It's the hard that makes it great."

Researchers in California reported on a study where amoebas were placed in separate tanks. In one tank the conditions were perfect—temperature, humidity, water level, and other elements were monitored constantly to provide an environment most conducive to growth. In the other tank the amoebas were subjected to variations in temperature, fluid level, and other extreme conditions. To everyone's surprise the amoebas in the tank with ideal conditions died faster than those subjected to harsh conditions. Having things too easy, too comfortable, too soft, can cause decay and deterioration. Being forced to adapt and change can actually lead to growth.

Sometimes it's good to have an obstacle to overcome, whether in football or anything. When things go bad we usually rise to the occasion.

—Vincent T. Lombardi

Motivating Others

Getting your people to move, to act, to risk, or to change isn't easy. Your challenge as a coach is to motivate your team. There are three ways to motivate:

- By fear and coercion (the "or else" method)
- By incentives (the "carrot on the stick" method)
- By persuasion and inspiration

Fear and Coercion

You can get short-term results motivating by fear and coercion. You tell your people, do it, "or else"—or else you'll be reprimanded, punished, or fired. If your world view is that people are lazy and unreliable, this is probably how you choose to motivate people. This is an easy way to get

Those convinced against their will are of the same opinion still.
—Dale Carnegie

people moving and doesn't require a lot of effort on your part.

The directors of a medium-sized company implemented a profit-sharing plan. Every employee had to sign up before the plan could be implemented. Everyone did, except John, a warehouseman. John didn't think the plan would benefit him, so he refused to sign up. His fellow employees begged, wheedled, and cajoled, all to no avail. John was unmoved. Finally, the company president called John into his office and said, "John, here's a pen, here's the profit-sharing plan. Sign it, *or else* I'm going to have to let you go." Without a moment's hesitation, John grabbed the pen and signed. As he was leaving the president stopped him. "John, do you mind telling me why it took you so long to sign?" John answered, "Nobody explained it quite so clearly before."

Effective as it can be, the "or else" method has definite drawbacks. People who feel they're being pushed by do it "or else" will resist and push back, by procrastination, sloppy work, absenteeism, and a lack of pride in their work. For these people, pushing back—creative avoidance—is a way to maintain their dignity and becomes more important than accomplishing the goal. And the minute the "or else" factor is removed, the minute you stop pushing, these people will respond to the absence of coercion very quickly—they will lie down and quit on you.

Coaches and leaders who motivate this way—my father included—discover that after a period of time, their people begin to turn a deaf ear to the coercion. They have heard the threats and the "or elses" so often that it becomes meaningless to them. My father stepped down as coach of the Packers for a number of reasons. One reason, I believe, is that he found it increasingly difficult to motivate his players, many of whom had been with him for seven and eight

Force is all conquering, but its victories are short lived.
—Abraham Lincoln

years and had heard all the "or elses" too many times.

Incentives

Dangle some incentives in front of most people and they will move. Many sales organizations have had success with this type of motivation. But it carries with it the seeds of its own ineffectiveness. The problem is that you must constantly increase the size of the carrot. Sooner or later people perceive the reward not as a reason to move, but as simply their due for doing their job in an ordinary fashion. Remove the incentive, and many of these people will stop dead in their tracks. In the short term, incentives will get people moving. But in the long run, incentives can actually lead to a deterioration in performance.

The use of incentives to motivate people runs directly counter to getting people to work together as a team. Incentives cause people to focus on the "carrot" instead of service, quality, and innovation. Incentive-driven people are averse to risk. They will do nothing except those things that will assure them gaining the incentive.

Today's professional football player is bigger, faster, and stronger than his counterpart of the 1960s and 1970s. So the game should be better, right? In my opinion, it isn't. If anything, pro football today is sloppier, with more mistakes and mediocrity. Why? Because the majority of the players are motivated to play principally for the money, and the money is so great that more traditional forms of motivation— pride in performance, pursuit of excellence for excellence's sake—is lost on these players. The players lack focus and they aren't dedicated to playing the game to the best of their ability. Whatever your profession, if you made the mistakes in your line of work that we see on Sunday afternoon, you'd be unemployed.

We work to become, not to acquire.
—Elbert Hubbard

Today a player's principal motivation is to avoid injury and extend his career for as long as possible.

Nikita Khrushchev, Soviet Premier from 1958 to 1964, was once quoted as saying, "Call it what you will, incentives are the only way to make people work harder." That kind of approach did wonders for the Russian economy, didn't it?

Persuasion and Inspiration

As we said earlier, getting people to move isn't easy. Change is difficult; there must be some juice, some emotion, some inspiration to cause people to take action.

Persuasion and inspiration help people motivate themselves. Today's successful coaches don't coerce or bribe, they persuade and inspire. For each player they paint a picture of the pay value, the personal profitability to the player, in helping the team accomplish the overall goal. Then there's a magnetic draw to the end result.

Does this mean that to be a successful coach you need to have charisma and be a great speaker? Those qualities would certainly help, but they are not essential. Inspiration lies in enthusiasm, energy, and commitment. As a coach you must promote your vision and persuade your team members to give their best effort. Most of your people, down deep, want more than just a job. Most of them want a career, because their spirit, their will, is bigger than a 9-to-5 job that yields just a paycheck. As their coach, you must help your people find a greater sense of purpose and meaning than their day-to-day existence on the job.

This kind of motivation is more difficult to implement and takes more time and energy. But this motivation can be permanent and self-generating. To motivate this way, paradoxically, we first have to concede that we probably can't truly

It is better to have a lion at the head of an army of sheep than a sheep at the head of an army of lions.

—Confucius

Leadership is a word and a concept that has been more argued than almost any other I know . . . I would rather try to persuade a man to go along, because once I have persuaded him he will stick. If I scare him, he will stay as long as he is scared, and then he is gone.

—Dwight D. Eisenhower

motivate anyone other than ourselves. Motivation is internal, an inside-out process, a do-it-yourself project. Charles Garfield, the author of *Peak Performance* and other books, says it this way: *"The most powerful human motivator of all is the desire to be proud of ourselves in the pursuit of something we care about deeply."*

What you as a coach must do is create an environment and an atmosphere within which your people can motivate themselves, by doing something they care about deeply, and doing it well.

It's not likely you can change the kind of business your company is engaged in. But what you can do is help your people see the worth and importance of what they do. Good coaches paint great pictures for their people, graphic portraits of the pay value, the personal profitability of the job or task at hand. Then it's no longer, "I have to do it or else." Now, it's "I want to. I choose to, I like it, this is my idea." This is intrinsic motivation, people doing things because they *want* to.

My wife and I have four children. The youngest, Joseph, played football for the Air Force Academy at 6 feet 3 inches and 230 pounds. Clearly, a strong back any yardworker could use. But when Joe was a teenager I could never get him to help. Working in the yard was a "have to," and he always had an excuse—practice, study, other commitments. One day though, I was working in the yard and who should appear, unsummoned, ready to work, gloves and all, but Joe. You could have knocked me over with a feather. Then I remembered. The day before we had purchased a new backboard and Joe knew instinctively, "If I help the old man with the yard work, he'll help me put up the backboard." Working in the yard, this one time, was a "want to."

In the movie *Chariots of Fire* a group of track and field athletes were competing against one another to represent Great Britain in the

I don't believe in team motivation. I believe in getting a team prepared so that it knows it will have the necessary confidence when it steps on the field and be prepared to play a good game.
—Tom Landry

When you reach for the stars, you may not quite get one, but you won't come up with a handful of mud either.
—Leo Burnett

Reach beyond your grasp. Your goals should be grand enough to get the best of you.
—Teilhard de Chardin

1924 Olympics. One of the athletes was Harold Abrahamson, whose chief competition for a place on the team was a fellow from Scotland. After the Scot beat Abrahamson in some of the preliminary races, Abrahamson, feeling sorry for himself, whined to his girlfriend, "If I can't win, I won't run." She looked at Abrahamson and said *"If you won't run, you can't win."*

This is a lesson most of us have been forced to learn, but seemingly we don't want those around us to learn it. Rather, we seek to insulate our people from the frustration and disappointment that comes from missing a goal. "Don't bite off more than you can chew," we tell them. "Be happy with what you've got."

What baloney! Teach your people to bite off more than they can chew. Encourage your people to reach for the stars. Whatever the result, they'll come away with a whole lot more than they would have otherwise, and they will relearn a very valuable lesson. A lesson too many of us have forgotten:

Without turmoil and commotion,
*   there is no growth.*

Without turmoil and commotion,
*   there is no change.*

Without turmoil and commotion,
*   there is no improved performance.*

Good coaches understand these dynamics and see it as a challenge, not a threat—they make it work for them, not against them.

My father's motivational technique was more fear and coercion than anything else. He could pound a bump on your head. Vince Lombardi's attitude was "My way or the highway" and he allowed his players no illusions about the permanence of their employment. "If you can't get the job done I'll find someone who can," he would say.

He once told his players, in one of those turns of a phrase that has survived the years, "If you are not fired with enthusiasm, you will be fired with enthusiasm."

But in the closed universe of pro football, in a different time than now, he really had a hammer! There was no one else for the players to look to. He was the first authority, and the last. How many of you have that kind of a hammer today? And if you had it, would you be inclined to use it?

Today an entire industry of *rights* has sprung up. With OSHA, the EPA, unions, arbitrators, and human rights laws dealing with age, sex, and race discrimination, do it "or else" doesn't get people moving anymore. They either don't know what you're talking about, or don't care. The "or else" is that you, the coach, have to do it yourself or persuade and inspire others to care and to do it.

Yes, Vince Lombardi could pound a bump on your head. Yet once he had your attention with do it "or else," he would wisely slide into a more persuasive form of motivation.

Jerry Kramer, an All-Pro guard for the Packers for many years and the author of the best-seller *Instant Replay,* tells of a time early in his career when he was having a terrible time during a goal line scrimmage. He was jumping offside, missing assignments. My father got in Jerry's face. (Jerry was six-foot-three; on a good day, my father was five-ten; but my father had a forefinger about 10 inches long and 2 inches wide.) My father yelled at Jerry, "Mister, the attention span for a grade school kid is 30 seconds, a high school kid a minute, and for a college kid, 3 minutes. Mister, where does that leave you?"

Kramer says he left practice totally discouraged, giving serious thought to quitting. In the locker room, my father sized up the situation immediately, walked over to Jerry, tousled his

Some players you pat on their butts, some players you kick their butts, some players you leave alone.
—Pete Rose

There's no hereditary strata in leading. They're not born; they're made. There has to be an inclination, a commitment, a willing-ness to command.
—Vincent T. Lombardi

The leader can never close the gap between himself and the group. If he does he is no longer what he must be. He must walk a tightrope between the consent he must win and the control he must exert.
—Vincent T. Lombardi

hair, and told him, "Son, someday you're going to be one of the greatest guards in football." Jerry Kramer will tell you that from that point on as a football player, he never had to be pushed again. From that point on, his sole motivation was to fulfill the vision my father had painted for him. And in my opinion, Jerry Kramer went on to become one of the greatest guards in football.

I'm not saying it has to be one way or the other, coercive or persuasive. Do it "or else" is a pretty good way to get people moving short-term. My question for you as a coach is, where's the balance?

Inspiration lies in action. You must walk your talk. You don't inspire by ability or talent. You inspire your people by your willingness to take action that dramatizes your commitment.

You inspire your people by being involved, by spending time in the trenches. You inspire people through your participation in the ebb and flow of your organization. It is a cardinal mistake for a coach to become isolated and out of touch with the everyday activities of the team.

Commitment, Attitude, and Tradition

A man can be as great as he wants to be. If you believe in yourself and have the courage, the determination, the dedication, the competitive drive and if you are willing to sacrifice the little things and pay the price for the things that are worthwhile, it can be done. Once a man has made a commitment to a way of life, he puts the greatest strength in the world behind him. It's something we call heart power. Once a man has made this commitment, nothing will stop him short of success.

—Vincent T. Lombardi

My father was a deeply religious man. He went to mass and communion on a daily basis. Yet he never considered a championship to be a sign of divine favor. Rather, in my father's eyes, a championship was clear evidence that a few people—working closely together in a spirit of discipline, singleness of purpose, and a commitment to excellence—could win no matter how the odds were stacked against them.

In less emotional terms, I'd put it this way— the players my father coached were not a loose collection of individuals. They were a team! The Green Bay Packers had synergy.

1 + 1 didn't = 2.
1 + 1 = 4, 8, 16!

On the Green Bay Packers, as with all winning teams, the whole was bigger than the sum of the parts. The Green Bay Packers trusted one another, they respected one another, they were committed to one another—and yes, if you're comfortable with the term, they loved one another.

Trust—I know I can count on you to do what you say you will do.

Respect—I value you, so you can count on me to do what I say I will do.

My father said, *"The quality of a person's life is in direct proportion to their commitment to excellence."*

What is this thing, commitment, that can define the quality of your life? Think about the last time you made a commitment. Perhaps it was when you were promoted to manager and you promised the boss to whip the department into shape. Perhaps it was when you got married, and promised—here's a commitment—to love and honor, until death.

When we commit to something we make a strong, firm decision to do it. Thus, at the very heart of commitment is the act of making a

Teamwork is what the Green Bay Packers were all about. They didn't do it for individual glory. They did it because they loved one another.
—Vincent T. Lombardi

Always do what you say you are going to do. It is the glue and fiber that binds successful relationships.
—Jeffrey Timmons

Nothing binds us one to another like a promise kept, nothing divides us like a promise broken.
—Mass Mutual

You've got to give loyalty down, if you want loyalty up.
—Donald T. Regan

decision. The Latin root for decision is to "cut away from," as in incision.

When we commit to something, we "cut away" all the other possibilities and options. When we commit to something, we "cut away" all the excuses, all the rationalizations. Without commitment we lack the focus to achieve things. There is no focus if we have other options and possibilities. There is no focus if we have excuses available to us.

We have forty million reasons . . . but not a single excuse.
—Rudyard Kipling

Sun Tzu, an ancient Chinese general, grasped this principle centuries ago when he wrote a book called *The Art of War*. Sun Tzu warned that if you have your enemy's army cornered, leave them a way out. Because if you corner your enemy's army and don't leave them a way out, they will fight to the death and you will get more than you bargained for, because you'll be facing a truly committed army. Commitment is leaving yourself "no way out." Commitment is, figuratively at least, being willing to "fight to the death" for what you've committed to.

Cortez, the Spanish explorer, didn't know Sun Tzu. The two men were separated by many miles and many years. But Cortez grasped Sun Tzu's understanding of commitment. When Cortez first landed in the New World, he obtained the commitment of his conquistadors rather dramatically, something he learned from the ancient Greeks. He landed, unloaded his ships, and then he burned them right down to the waterline, leaving his people "no way out"—no way back to Spain, no other options, no other possibilities—so they might as well commit to pushing ahead!

You don't need to be a fight fan to learn from the well-known manager and trainer of some years ago, Cus D'Amato. He managed a good heavyweight champion by the name of Floyd Patterson. D'Amato once had a fighter who had been in training for quite a while. A sportswriter asked D'Amato, "Is your boy ready?" D'Amato answered, "About 90 percent" The sportswriter said "What's the matter, this guy's been in training for months, how come he's not ready?" D'Amato answered, "I don't believe a fighter ever gets in the ring thinking he's 100 percent. If he does and gets beat, he'll never get in the ring again."

Most of us have a tendency to do this, to hedge our commitments, both individually and as a team. We pursue our goals with about a 90 percent effort, so that if we get beat, if we lose, we've got that 10 percent to make an excuse with, 10 percent to rationalize with.

Commitment means having no reserve portion. Commitment is 100 percent effort, 100 percent of the time. Commitment is burning our ships to the waterline. Commitment is, figuratively at least, being willing to "fight to the death" for what we've committed to.

Does 100 percent effort, 100 percent of the time sound a bit extreme to you? See what a 99.9 percent effort will get you:

- 18 major plane crashes each day around the world
- Doctors operating on the wrong patient 500 times each day
- 17,000 pieces of mail lost by the U.S. Postal Service every hour
- Two million documents lost by the IRS this year
- 291 pacemaker operations performed incorrectly this year
- 20,000 incorrect drug prescriptions written in the next 12 months
- 114,500 mismatched pairs of shoes shipped this year
- 107 incorrect medical procedures performed by the end of today

Until one is committed, there is hesitancy, the chance to draw back, always ineffectiveness. Concerning all acts of initiative, there is one elementary truth, the ignorance of which kills countless ideas and splendid plans. That the moment one definitely commits oneself, then providence moves, too. All sorts of things occur to help one that would never otherwise have occurred.
—William C. Murray

In 1987 the National Football League players went on strike. Players on the picket line assured interviewers of their total commitment to the strike and their intent to hold fast to their demands whatever the cost. However, the NFL owners were committed, too. The owners' commitment took the form of continuing to play the games without the regular players, with anybody they could dig up. The quality of football suffered, but so did the striking players. Within a matter of weeks, the players slowly returned to their teams. The trickle of strike defectors became a torrent and the NFL Players Association called off the strike. In 1987, the NFL players lacked commitment. They weren't willing to "fight to the death" for what they believed in. Unlike Cortez and his soldiers, the NFL players kept their options open.

Without commitment, all the rest—goals, vision, mission and purpose—amount to nothing more than a good idea! For here's the kicker: if you lack focus, if you are still keeping your options open—you can't commit to it! Unless your goals are vivid, clear, and precise, you can't bring to the table the awesome power of commitment!

So my question is to you, regarding your goal, your vision, your mission:

Can you taste it?

Can you touch it?

Can you smell it?

Can you see it?

Do you know what it's going to sound like, coming down the hallway?

Don't make your commitments lightly—individually or organizationally. Because along with the power of commitment comes the struggle, the pain, and the discomfort of commitment.

There's been much written and said about the

spartan discipline and the singleness of purpose my father demanded of his players. If I could boil down to one phrase what my father stood for, it would be:

To accomplish anything worthwhile you must pay the price.

You must pay the price to win; by definition, success is paying the price. Commitment is the willingness to pay the price of pain and discomfort. To win, to achieve, to excel—it's not a matter of luck, of catching a break. It's not a matter of timing—being in the right place at the right time. To achieve, you must understand a simple law of physics—*cause and effect.* To excel, you must understand and practice a simple law of nature—*you reap what you sow.* There are no short cuts. There's a price to be paid to accomplish anything worthwhile, and that price comes in terms of planning and preparation, sacrifice and self-denial, effort and hard work and persistence and perseverance.

Everybody, sooner or later, sits down to a banquet of consequences.

—Robert Louis Stevenson

Every team has a few players who by their attitude and habits drag down the team's overall performance. They ignore curfews and training rules, drink or engage in recreational drugs, and do other things that diminish their effort and performance. If team members lack commitment, their attitude will be: "Who am I to tell someone else how to live his life?"

But when the team comes to understand the vision and is committed to it, they won't tolerate the type of behavior that detracts from the team's performance. They will take it upon themselves to shape up the player who isn't doing his part. Winning sports teams apply this type of peer pressure in the locker room—every day.

The Packers' success during my father's years had many keys—including trust, respect and commitment. One factor critical to their success was their winning attitude. When the Green Bay

Packers stepped on the field, they didn't just hope to win, they *expected* to win!

A game in 1962 against the Detroit Lions was a case in point. The Lions played magnificently that day, and held the ball and a 7-6 lead with less than a minute to play. A running play and a punt would pretty much seal the win for the Lions. But the Lion quarterback inexplicably chose to pass. Herb Adderley intercepted, Paul Hornung kicked a field goal, and Green Bay won a game a lesser team would have resigned itself to losing.

Once in a while the Packers lost a game. They could have explained the setback by saying they hadn't played their best, or they didn't get the breaks. But the team had the essential ingredient of *all* winning teams: they saw themselves as winners. When the final score didn't support their belief, the Packers explained the loss by saying they simply ran out of time.

All successful teams—all winning organizations—have this kind of attitude. When they make a sales presentation, when they sit around a conference table to solve a production problem, they don't *hope* to make the sale, they don't *hope* to solve the problem. Winners *expect* to make the sale, they *expect* to solve the problem.

A winning attitude is the cornerstone for a winning tradition, an asset all successful teams possess. A winning tradition exists when new people join your company and find themselves indoctrinated by the old hands, the veterans—by word and deed—into the prevailing attitude and behavior: "This is how we do things around here, around here we *expect* to win."

Good coaches create an environment within which trust, respect, and commitment can flourish. They engender within their team a winning attitude that they then help transform into a winning tradition. Now, you don't just win on Sunday, or you don't just make your sales goals

Every time I stepped on the field, I believed my team was going to walk off the field the winner, somehow, someway.

—Roger Staubach

Second place is meaningless. You can't always be first, but you have to believe you should have been—time just runs out on you.

—Vincent T. Lombardi

this quarter. Now, the expectation that you will win every time becomes part of your corporate culture. Your team believes they will win year after year, time after time. This is the real payoff for coaching for teamwork.

What do you suppose comes first? Do we have trust and respect and commitment for one another and then we win? Or once we're winning is it just easier to overlook one another's differences? Kind of a chicken and egg question, isn't it? Some people will tell you that results precede attitude—that first we experience some success, then people's attitude begins to change.

Based on my observation, success and attitude have to follow parallel courses. Certainly, you need victories to reinforce the changes you're trying to make. But if you're looking for those breakthrough victories you need a collective change in attitude. And it's not just the victories; sometimes it's a loss or setback that provides a coach with the greatest opportunity to affect attitudes.

What I try to do, is create an environment in which it's possible to succeed. Football is a constant education. I present ideas, not mandates, and try to take advantage of the good people we have. A good coach has to constantly adjust.
—*George Seifert*

It's easy to have faith in yourself and have discipline when you're a winner, when you're number one. What you've got to have is faith and discipline when you're not yet a winner.
—*Vincent T. Lombardi*

The Winning Team

Snowflakes are one of nature's most fragile things, but just look what they can do when they stick together.

—Vesta M. Kelly

A Little League coach called over one of his players. He asked the boy, "Do you understand what teamwork is?" The little boy nodded yes. "Do you understand that win or lose, we do it together as a team?" The little boy nodded yes. "So," the coach continued, "when a strike is called, or you're called out at first, you don't swear and curse and attack the umpire . . . do you understand all that?" The little boy nodded yes. "Good," said the coach. "Now go over there and explain it to your mother."

In my 30 years of experience in the world of sports and business, I've observed many teams both on the playing field and in numerous office settings. Winning teams come in all shapes and sizes and vary tremendously in their composition. Despite the variations, the successful teams I've been around have exhibited five distinct characteristics:

1. The team collectively determines what end result it wants to achieve and how it will achieve it.

People who work together will win, whether it be against complex football defenses, or the complex problems of modern society.

—Vincent T. Lombardi

77

2. Team members understand how accomplishing the team's goals will help them achieve their individual goals (each individual understands "what's in it for me").

3. Team members see how their individual efforts contribute to the overall success of the team and accept personal accountability for the success of the team.

4. The team is mentally tough, able to rise each time it falls.

5. The team makes its vision an absolute part of its belief system.

Let's examine each of these characteristics.

Determine the Vision Collectively

Winning teams *collectively* determine the end result they want to achieve and how they will achieve it—the process of goal setting. We're not talking profit, bottom line, or market share. These things are very important, but what we're talking about here is deeper, more basic—*mission, purpose, vision.* The process requires answers to questions that cut to the very heart of the way you think about your work. Why do you get out of bed in the morning? Why do you and your people come to work in the morning? Where do you want to be six months from now, a year, five years from now, as far as your employees and customers are concerned? Who is your customer? What precisely does your customer value? What are the needs of the marketplace that you want to fulfill? What exactly is your business? What was the initial vision for your company, and is it still valid? Should it be reexamined? What drives you? What motivates you? What gives your work purpose? What gives your work meaning?

Eighty percent of American managers cannot answer with any measure of confidence these seemingly simple questions: What is my job? What in it really counts? How well am I doing?

—W. Edward Deming

The business that we love, we rise betime and go to it with delight.

—William Shakespeare

Several years ago I spoke to the employees of a successful waste disposal company. Waste disposal is a fancy name for getting rid of garbage. Anyone who has lived in an urban area knows that getting the garbage picked up—efficiently and on time—makes a big difference in a city's quality of life. (I've been in places when the garbage haulers were on strike, and it's not a pretty sight—or smell.)

But let's face it, few of us regard waste collection as a business with a vision—but this company had one. Its top people were committed to helping their community maintain a clean, healthy environment. Employees were trained not only in the basics of their job, but they were also educated to the big picture, the *reason* for their job. They were shown *why* waste collection was essential to good environmental practices. Workers attended monthly meetings to brainstorm on problems and share solutions.

This decision of "what end result do we want to achieve," the vision, is *collectively* arrived at. Everyone has input, everyone has a say. People know more about their job than their boss or any expert. *People closest to the job know best how to do their job.*

I'm not suggesting you take a vote or that you run a democracy at your workplace, but this is how you build commitment. You can't ask people to commit to a vision or give 100 percent to a mission if they haven't had a hand in determining the mission or vision. But if your people feel they've been listened to and that they've had a say in formulating the vision, then it's *their* idea, so they have an investment in the end result. And at that point they'll give their commitment, not before.

Let me try to illustrate this commitment concept. What are you, as a coach and a leader, interested in first and foremost? Results, of course! Sometimes we can't quantify these

All decisions should be made as low as possible in the organization. The Charge of the Light Brigade was ordered by an officer who wasn't there looking at the territory.
—Robert Townsend

People support what they help create.
—Anonymous

When you identify with your company's purpose, when you experience ownership in a shared vision, you find yourself doing your life's work instead of just doing time.
—John Naisbitt and Patricia Aburdene

results, but nevertheless in everything we do, we're looking for an end product—results. Two factors determine the results you achieve as a coach—the *decisions* you make, singly or collectively, and the *execution* of those decisions. Let's get a little more sophisticated and say it's the *quality of the decision* and the *commitment behind the execution* of the decision that determines your results. We could illustrate this in a formula:

Quality of the Decision x Commitment Behind the Execution of the Decision = Result

Let's assume we can quantify both the decision and its execution on a scale of 1 to 10, 10 being the best.

Pretend you want to institute a new marketing plan for your company. So you get together with a few of your trusted associates and you come up with a new marketing plan. Because you're good, let's give your decision a 9. Now you go to your marketing people and inform them of your decision and show them how to execute it. Guess what their reaction will be? "That's *their* idea!" they'll say, and it won't be a compliment. Some of your people will be less than enthusiastic about your plan. Some will wonder why you didn't ask them for their input; they may show remarkable creativity in shooting holes in your carefully designed marketing plan. Most likely, they will probably commit to your decision, without enthusiasm—at about a 3. The result would look like this: **9 x 3 = 27.**

When your people fail to buy into the decision, it's "your" idea, and they withhold their commitment. Then in times of stress or pressure they will take the path of least resistance and do things "their" way, rather than the way that's consistent with achieving the end result.

Late in the fourth quarter, with his team

Never tell people how to do things. Tell them what to do and they will surprise you with their ingenuity.
—George S. Patton

needing 10 yards for a crucial first down, a wide receiver—tired and feeling the pressure—will cut his pattern off at 9 yards, rather than take the hit from the defensive back he knows is coming if he runs his pattern a yard deeper. He'll make the catch, but failing to run his pattern correctly, he will fail to pick up the first down and his team will be forced to give up the ball.

This is what my father was driving at when he said, *"Fatigue makes cowards of us all."* When your people are tired or stressed, they will take the easy way out—unless and until you have achieved total commitment to the end result.

Let's go back and change the story. Instead of making the decision yourself, you get your marketing staff involved. They kick the problem around and finally decide on a marketing plan. Let's say it's not a decision you would have made. You can only give it a 7. But it has something going for it. Because everyone had a hand in the decision, it's now *their* idea. What do you imagine their attitude and the level of their commitment will be now? Yes! Your people are not going to allow this decision to be anything but a success—after all, it's *their* decision. So they commit to the execution of the decision at a much higher level—perhaps a 7. Now the result is: **7 x 7 = 49.**

Almost twice the result!

What result do you prefer? That depends on whether you, as a coach, are end result oriented or whether you're more interested in who gets the credit and who is in control.

Once you determine the end result you want to achieve, then you must determine how you're going to achieve it. For it's the "How" that separates the successful teams from everybody else. The end result is like the final score. I've never seen a team win a game looking at the scoreboard. It's the "How"—the strategies and tactics to achieve the vision—that determines the winners.

As a rule of thumb, involve everyone in everything.
—Tom Peters

There's no way, through this book, to tell you specifically how to achieve the end results you want, for that would depend on the nature of your particular business. However, there are some general guidelines for accomplishing the "How" and the end results you want. From my experience your approach should be threefold:

1. Train your people in the fundamentals.

2. Keep the lines of communication open.

3. Build commitment within your organization.

Number one, you've got to stick to the fundamentals. What are the fundamentals in your business? In football, it's blocking and tackling. Are you spending time, effort, and money on training and retraining your people in the fundamentals? Every summer, last year's Super Bowl champion returns to training camp and begins by relearning the fundamentals of football. If they can, can't you? Ken Blanchard and Spencer Johnson, in their book *The One Minute Manager,* point out that most companies spend 50 to 70 percent of their money on staff salaries, and less than 10 percent of their budget to train their people. *The One Minute Manager* was written in 1981, and things have changed since then. But have they changed in your organization? Training can't be treated as a fringe benefit. Training— properly targeted, presented, and evaluated—will flow straight to your bottom line.

Peter Drucker says, when it comes to successful organizations, it's not so much a matter of doing things right; it's doing the right things. Actually, it's a combination of the two. So again, are you spending time, effort, and money on training and retraining your people in doing the right things right, so they do the right things right—instinctively, habitually, without even thinking about it? Does your training program

No system is any good if the players are not well grounded in the fundamentals.

—John Wooden

cause your people to work in a relaxed, natural, and free-flowing manner? Because we all know how effective we can be when we're relaxed, natural, and free-flowing.

Without training, they lacked knowledge.
Without knowledge, they lacked confidence.
Without confidence, they lacked victory.
                                    —*Julius Caesar*

Communication is so important, it's dealt with in a separate chapter. To repeat, communication must flow both ways: top-down and bottom-up.

The third component of the "How" is commitment—getting your people to give 100 percent effort 100 percent of the time. "How do I do that?" you ask. Through training and communication. Nothing will convince your people more that you care for them than training. Few companies can promise lifetime employment to their people. But through training, a company can insure people lifetime employability. There's the truism: "They don't care how much you know until they know how much you care." The one thing that will convince your people that you care for them is your investment in their training. If your people believe you care for them and their future, they will give you their commitment.

If you will invest in training your people in the fundamentals, if you will keep the lines of communication open, top-down and bottom-up, and if you will build commitment within your organization, you'll rarely have to look at the scoreboard to see how you're doing. You'll know.

See the Pay Value

The second characteristic of a winning team is that everyone asks themselves, "What's in it for me?" "Where's the pay value, the personal profitability in this for me?" This isn't selfish, this is human nature. I hope you aren't laboring

People may doubt what you say, but they always believe what you do.
                  —*Unknown*

Invest in human capital as much as in hardware. Use training as a vehicle for instilling a strategic trust.
                  —*Tom Peters*

Build for your team a feeling of oneness, of dependence upon one another, and of strength to be derived from unity.
                  —*Vincent T. Lombardi*

under the illusion that your people are working for you or your company. *They're not.* They are working for themselves. "This is my job, this is my career, my profession." This is why training is so important. We're all basically entrepreneurial. There may be a whole lot of reasons why we're not working for ourselves, but that doesn't change the fact that we're entrepreneurial at heart.

When the Green Bay Packers set out in pursuit of the Super Bowl, each of them sought it for their own individual reasons. Many of the players wanted to pick up the winner's check; for some, the prestige of wearing a Super Bowl ring was paramount. Some of the younger players, perhaps more so now than back then, may have thought, "If we win the Super Bowl, I'll be very big in the singles bars."

If that's where your people are coming from, then that's where you have to deal with them. We're talking about motivation again. Earlier, we pointed out that the essence of motivation is gestalt, the tension between what we've got and what we want. To motivate your team you must communicate your clear, precise vision to them. Then you must show each individual how they can get what they want by helping the team get what it wants. *Coaching is the process of bringing together a diverse group of people to accomplish a common end result for a variety of different reasons.*

If your imagination leads you to understand how quickly people grant your requests when those requests appeal to their self-interest, you can have practically anything you go after.

—Napoleon Hill

How is it with your team, your organization? Have you taken the time to find out why your people are coming to work in the morning? Some want to pick up a paycheck. Their interest is in making money and supporting their family. Others are interested in a career, where they can measure their progress through their promotions and their growing salary. Many of the people working for you are looking for a *calling*, something that will give meaning and purpose to their lives.

And once you understand why your people are coming to work, have you painted a picture for them, showing them how they can get what they want by helping the team get what it wants? Or are your people still coming to work on a "have to" basis, with all of the push-back and resistance that goes along with I have to do it, "or else".

Build Accountability

The third quality common to winning teams is the willingness of everyone on the team to accept accountability. Everyone asks themselves, "What do I need to do, in terms of habits, attitudes, and skills to help us win our version of the Super Bowl?"

In a football context, this is easy to see. The linemen, this week, need to control the line of scrimmage, protect the quarterback, and pick up the blitz on third and long. For this game, the running backs need to gain 150 yards among them, hold on to the ball, no fumbles, and they need to catch enough passes underneath to keep the linebackers honest. The quarterback knows, this Sunday, he must throw for at least 200 yards, avoid interceptions, and he needs to take his team in for at least 27 points. For this game, the defense has for its goal to cause three turnovers and limit the opposing team to 17 points.

Taken in isolation these things don't mean a thing. But when you put it all together, it fits like a puzzle, a mosaic. Now, you've got the game plan, the big picture, the vision. Everyone has a hand in putting together the game plan. They buy into it, they commit to it, and then they see how their individual effort contributes to achieving the game plan. When everyone does their part, you win this Sunday, next Sunday, and pretty soon you're in contention for the Super Bowl.

You can get everything in life you want, if you help enough other people get what they want.

—Zig Ziglar

The achievements of an organization are the results of the combined effort of each individual.

—Vincent T. Lombardi

Everyone has a hand in putting together the game plan. They buy into it, they commit to it, and then they see how their individual effort contributes to achieving the game plan. This is how you, as a coach, build accountability, how you get your people to truly care about their work.

If people fail to see the connection between their individual effort and achieving the team's mission, performance will deteriorate. The airplane mechanic must understand that the ultimate goal is a happy traveler who will fly her airline again—not simply getting the plane serviced. A claims adjustor needs to focus on a satisfied customer who will buy his company's products again—not just getting the claim settled.

Two stonemasons were chipping some blocks out of granite. When asked what they were doing, one replied, "I'm cutting granite into blocks." The other said, "I'm building a cathedral."

They were both right of course, but the first stonemason didn't understand the game plan, and saw only the granite before him. The second stonemason understood the game plan and he saw where his individual effort contributed to the game plan. It's a sure bet the second stonemason was a more productive worker.

How is it in your company? Is everyone aware of the game plan? Does everyone understand the big picture? Do people in sales, production, and administration understand how their individual efforts contribute to the game plan, the vision?

What we're talking about are ways to persuade people to accept accountability for their work, to "really care about the way things are going on around here." As a coach, you need to do three things to build accountability within your team:

1. Tell your people what you expect from them.

2. Give your people everything they need to do their job.

3. Get out of their way.

First, you need to tell your people precisely what you expect of them. Don't ask people to take accountability for their work if they don't know what's expected of their work. I'm not suggesting you cross the "t's" and dot the "i's" with respect to their job description. My question to you is: *Have you painted a picture for your people of what's it going to look like when they've done their job excellently?*

Wes Roberts in his book *Leadership Secrets of Attila the Hun* points out, "Chieftains must teach their Huns well that which is expected of them. Otherwise, Huns will probably do something not expected of them." And don't ask your people if they understand what they're supposed to do. They will always say yes. Rather, ask them to *tell you* what they're supposed to do. Very quickly you'll know—if they know.

The second thing you need to do to build accountability is to provide your people with everything they need to do their job—all the tools, of course, but the authority as well. You can't ask people to take accountability for their work if they lack the authority and the means to do their work. Accountability without authority breeds cynicism, and there is nothing more damaging to your team than cynicism seeping through the ranks.

> *If you want a person to do a job, give him authority and responsibility. If you want to do a job on a person, just give him the responsibility.*
> *—Gene Perret*

Finally, you need to give your people the freedom to do their job. Get out of their way—this includes letting them make mistakes

Few people go to work intending to perform poorly. Managers must show them how to pursue excellence.
—Unknown

Nothing is more pleasant than to know what's expected of you in life, in work, in love.
—Marlene Dietrich

and learn from their mistakes.

Sam Walton, the founder of Wal-Mart, made a speech to some students. Afterward, there was a question and answer session. A student asked, "To what do you attribute your success?" Walton said, "Good decisions." The student asked "What's it take to make good decisions?" Walton replied "Experience." Exasperated, the student persisted, "How do you get this experience?" Walton said, "Bad decisions."

No mistakes, no wisdom;
No experience, no wisdom.
—Stanley Goldstein

You have to allow people to do their work, and this includes allowing them to make some bad decisions so they can gain the experience to begin to make good decisions for you and your team.

An experienced horseman knows that when the trail gets difficult, it's best to give the horse its head. Left alone, the horse will find the best footing. As a coach, you've got to apply this same kind of philosophy to your team.

Good judgment is usually the result of experience and experience is usually the result of bad judgment.
—Robert Lovell

Years ago, pro football teams would bring a young quarterback along slowly. He would sit on the bench for a number of years and learn from the veteran playing ahead of him. No more. Today, with the intense pressure on coaches to win immediately and obtain quick results from the vast sums of money invested in the rookie quarterback, promising young quarterbacks are frequently inserted into the starting lineup too quickly. They absorb a lot of punishment and are made to shoulder the team's success or failure immediately. These young quarterbacks are not given the time or the freedom to make mistakes and learn from their mistakes. They become gun-shy and skittish, and often never develop their true potential. A number of teams are countering this by hiring quarterback coaches, whose only job is to teach and mentor the young QB through his mistakes.

Nordstrom, the Seattle-based department store, has a well-deserved reputation for service to the customer. They have set the standard for their industry. Nordstrom has only two short sentences in their employee manual. This is a prime example of allowing people the freedom to do their work.

Nordstrom Rules:

Rule #1: Use your good judgment in all situations. There will be no additional rules.

Mental Toughness

The fourth quality of a successful organization is mental toughness. Everyone asks themselves, "What may get in our way, what obstacles, what temporary setbacks might we face on the way to our version of the Super Bowl? Are we developing resiliency and mental toughness so that when these obstacles pop up, we'll just go over, around, or under, because nothing is going to stop us from achieving our vision."

The absolute number one characteristic of a winning team or organization is mental toughness, mental discipline—the ability to hold on to what you want, your goals, your vision, in the face of setbacks and adversity.

In the 1982 Winter Olympics in Albertville, France, a tiny figure skater from Japan, Midori Ito, provided a stirring example of mental toughness. Ito, not 5 feet tall, weighing around 100 pounds, was favored to win the gold medal, something no Japanese woman had ever done. She was carrying the expectations of her entire country on her back. Perhaps in response to this pressure, Ito and her coach decided to replace her trademark triple axel with an easier jump, the triple lutz, during her short program. Ito fell during the triple lutz, wiping out any chance she had at winning the gold medal.

Ito was perceived to have failed her entire country! But rather than allow the disappointment to defeat her, she bounced back and earned the silver medal. At the beginning of her long

The team that makes the most mistakes will probably win. The doer makes mistakes, and I want doers on my team, players who make things happen.
—John Wooden

Mental toughness is essential to success.
—Vincent T. Lombardi

You will find the extent of a man's determination on the goal line.
—Vincent T. Lombardi

The test of success is not what you do when you are on top. Success is how high you bounce when you hit bottom.
—George S. Patton

What counts is not the size of the dog in the fight—it's the size of the fight in the dog.
        —Dwight D. Eisenhower

No horse gets any-where until it is har-nessed. No steam or gas drives anything until it is confined. No Niagara ever turned into light and power until it is tunneled. No life ever grows great until it is focused, ded-icated, disciplined.
        —Harry Emerson Fosdick

Mental toughness is many things and rather difficult to explain. Its qualities are sacrifice and self-denial. Also most importantly, it is combined with the perfectly disciplined will, that refuses to give in. It's a state of mind—you could call it character in action.
        —Vincent T. Lombardi

program, Ito was in fourth place. She missed a triple axel early in her routine. At this point, Ito could have gone through the motions and skated off the ice, but not this woman. To the surprise of everyone, toward the conclusion of her routine when she was physically and mentally exhausted, Ito hit the triple axel and became the first woman ever to do so in the Olympics, thereby vaulting her from fourth to second place.

Mental toughness can come in a 5-foot, 100-pound package. You don't have to be a hulking linebacker or have a motorcycle and a leather jacket to be mentally tough.

Mental toughness is commitment, to the hundredth power. Mental toughness is tenacity and persistence in the face of obstacles and failure. Mental toughness is also focus, the ability to concentrate on the desired end result through the emotional highs and lows we all experience.

In 1960, my father's second season as coach, the Packers lost the NFL championship game to the Philadelphia Eagles. It was a devastating defeat for the Packers, who left the field knowing they were the better team and should have won the game. My father quickly called all the players together in the locker room. Without yelling or raising his voice, he told the players very deliberately, "Perhaps you didn't realize that you could have won this game. But I think there's no doubt in your minds now. And that's why you will win it all next year." Right there he provided the vision for the next season. With this vision clearly focused in their minds, the Packers won it all in 1961 and won it again in 1962 for good measure.

Much has been made of the Buffalo Bills losing four consecutive Super Bowls. Because of this failure in the ultimate game the team has been painted as a loser. Nothing could be further from the truth. If you are looking for an organization to model, look to the Buffalo Bills. Any other team, after losing the second Super Bowl, would have found an excuse not to contend for a third chance. The Bills not only came back a third time, they answered the bell for a fourth time.

The Buffalo Bills during those four years epitomized what mental toughness is all about—taking a hit and bouncing back up again and again—in the face of the current reality of ridicule, jokes, derision, and criticism.

The Bills' coach, Marv Levy, put it all in proper context:

"We've enjoyed our quest for the Super Bowl. It hasn't been an albatross around our necks or a glum Bataan death march. We've enjoyed fighting our way back and the opportunities. We've enjoyed the chance to assert we're the best team in football. We're not yet. That's our quest. But the journey is what's fun. If we win one, as satisfying as that would be, it wouldn't last as long as the enjoyment we'd derive out of getting there."

To win it, you must be in it.

—Darryl Talley, Buffalo Bills Player

How many organizations do you know of that would have had the focus, the commitment, and the mental discipline to accomplish what the Bills did? I have great admiration and respect for coach Marv Levy, his coaching staff, and the Bills players for what they achieved during those four years of triumph and trial.

A friend of mine, Lou Tice, says, "You move toward and become like that which you think about." What are you thinking about? What you've got, or what you want? You move toward your dominant picture. Your present thoughts determine your future.

What are you thinking about? What's your dominant picture? Where are your present thoughts? What are you focusing on? On what

Our achievements of today are but the sum total of the thoughts of yesterday. We are today where the thoughts of yesterday have brought us—and we will be tomorrow where the thoughts of today take us.

—Blaise Pascal

you've got, your problems? "Oh, the competition!" "Our margins are thin." "The economy is poor." "It's hard to get good people." "What are those politicians in Washington going to do to us next?"

Or are you thinking about what you want? Which very simply is, "What's it going to look like when we meet this challenge?" "What's it going to look like when we reach our goal?" "What's it going to look like when my dreams come true?"

Good coaches think about what they want. Their dominant picture is what they want. Their present thoughts are on what they want. Good coaches think future tense, as if the struggle is over, the mission is already accomplished! The sale is made, the deal is closed, the game is won, our quarterly goals are achieved.

Yes, you have to hustle, and yes, you have to strive, and yes, you have to work. But by now you know that because your goals are so clear, so vivid and so precise, because you are so focused, because you are so committed to your vision, you know that all it's going to take, is work, and some time, before your vision is achieved.

Mental toughness is the willingness, *day in and day out*, to keep the commitments you make to yourself. Mental toughness is the willingness, *day in and day out*, to walk your talk. Mental toughness is the willingness, *day in and day out*, to do the little things that separate the successful companies in your business from all the others. If you've been doing what you've been doing long enough, you know what those little things are!

How is it in your organization? Are you anticipating your setbacks in a proactive manner, or are you just reacting from crisis to crisis? What does it mean to be proactive? Let me give you the best example I've ever heard: You drive up to a red stoplight. Reactive is waiting for the light to turn green. Proactive is getting out of

You will become as small as your controlling desire, as great as your dominant aspiration.

—James Allen

Defeats are poison to some men. Great men have become mediocre because of their inability to accept and abide by a defeat. Many men have become great because they were able to rise above a defeat. If you achieve any kind of success and develop superior qualities as a man, chances are it will be because of the manner in which you meet the defeats that will come to you just as they come to all men.

—Unknown

your car, unscrewing the red bulb and replacing it with a green one.

Are you developing mental toughness and resiliency so that when these setbacks occur, you'll find a way to overcome? Or when adversity strikes, will your people throw up their hands in defeat and say, "Oh well, we didn't want that anyway."

Mental toughness is a learned trait; we aren't born with it or without it. You can engender mental toughness within your team. You do this by viewing every interaction, every success, every defeat as an opportunity to teach and reinforce your team's sense of resiliency, esteem, and toughness—its ability to take a hit and bounce right back up, its ability to rise each time it falls.

One of the tests of leadership is the ability to recognize a problem before it becomes an emergency.
—Arnold Glasgow

Where I am today has everything to do with the years I spent hanging on by my fingernails.
—Barbara Aronstein Black

The Race

Quit, give up, you're beaten,
they shout at me and plead,
There's just too much against you now,
this time you can't succeed.

And as I start to hang my head
in front of failure's face,
My downward fall is broken
by the memory of a race.

Perseverance is not a long race; it is many short races one after another.
—Walter Elliott

And hope refills my weakened will
as I recall that scene,
For just the thought of that short race
rejuvenates my being.

A child's race, young men, boys,
how I remember well,
Excitement sure, but also fear,
it wasn't hard to tell.

They all lined up so full of hope,
each thought to win the race,

Or tie for first, or if not that,
at least take second place.

And fathers watched from off the side,
each cheering for his son,
And each boy hoped to show his dad
that he would be the one.

The whistle blew, and off they went,
young hearts and hopes afire,
To win, to be the hero there,
was each young boy's desire.

And one boy in particular,
whose dad was in the crowd,
Was running in the lead and thought,
my dad will be so proud.

But as they speeded down the field
across a shallow dip,
The little boy who thought to win,
lost his step and slipped.

Trying hard to catch himself,
his hands flew out in brace,
And mid the laughter of the crowd,
he fell flat on his face.

So down he fell and with him hope,
he couldn't win, not now,
Embarrassed, sad, he only wished
to disappear somehow.

But as he fell his dad stood up,
and showed his anxious face,
Which to the boy so clearly said,
get up and win the race.

He quickly rose, no damage done,
behind a bit, that's all,
And ran with all his might and mind
to make up for his fall.

So anxious to restore himself,
    to catch up, to win,
His mind went faster than his legs,
    he slipped and fell again.

He wished then he had quit before,
    with only one disgrace,
I'm hopeless as a runner now,
    I shouldn't try to race.

But in the laughing crowd he searched,
    and found his father's face,
That steady look that said again,
    get up and win the race.

So up he jumped to try again,
    ten yards behind the last,
If I'm going to gain those yards,
    I've gotta move real fast.

Exerting everything he had
    he regained eight or ten,
But trying so hard to catch the lead,
    he slipped and fell again.

Defeat; he lay there silently,
    a tear dropped from his eye,
There's no sense in running anymore,
    three strikes I'm out, why try.

The will to rise had disappeared
    all hope had fled away,
So far behind, so error prone,
    I'll never go all the way.

I've lost—so what's the use he thought,
    I'll live with my disgrace,
But then he thought about his dad,
    who soon he'd have to face.

Get up—an echo sounded low,
    get up and take your place,
You were not meant for failure here,
    get up and win the race.

With borrowed will get up it said,
    you haven't lost at all,
**For winning is no more than this,
    to rise each time you fall.**

So up he rose to run once more,
    and with a new commit,
He resolved that win or lose the race,
    at least he wouldn't quit.

Three times he'd fallen, stumbling,
    three times he rose again,
Now he gave it all he had,
    and ran as though to win.

They cheered the winning runner
    as he crossed the line first place,
Head high and proud and happy,
    no failing, no falling, no disgrace.

But when the fallen youngster
    crossed the line last place,
The crowd gave him the greater cheer
    for finishing the race.

And even though he came in last
    with head bowed low unproud,
You would have thought he won the race
    to listen to the crowd.

And to his dad he sadly said,
    I didn't do so well,
To me you won, his father said
    you rose each time you fell.

And now when things seem dark and hard
and difficult to face,
The memory of that little boy
helps me in my race.

For all of life is like that race
with ups and downs and all,
**and all you have to do to win,
is rise each time you fall.**

Quit, give up, you're beaten,
they still shout in my face,
But another voice within me says,
get up and win the race.

—Unknown

This is an old story, but it bears repeating:

After World War II Winston Churchill gave the commencement address at his prep school, Harrow, where his academic record was less than outstanding. Churchill, one of the greatest orators in the world, walked up to the podium, looked over the crowd and said, "Never give up." He paused and said, "Never give up." He paused again and said, Never give up." That said, he sat down.

Incorporate Vision into Your Belief System

Finally, the fifth quality of all high-performance teams is that they make their vision, their purpose, an absolute part of their belief system. Winning teams are geared for the long haul. They believe in their vision, they take ownership of their vision. It's not an abstract idea; to them it's reality. When this year's Super Bowl champions set out, at the start of training camp, to win the Super Bowl, they won't just write it

The fourth dimension that determines success or failure is selfless teamwork and collective pride, which accumulate until they make positive thinking and victory habitual.
> *—Vincent T. Lombardi*

You have to have your heart in the business and the business in your heart.
> *—Thomas J. Watson, Sr.*

Involve all personnel at all levels in all functions in virtually everything.
> *—Tom Peters*

down—"Win the Super Bowl"—and go about their business. They will *live* the Super Bowl, they will *breathe* it, they will *talk about it all the time.* Before the season begins, they will visualize the Super Bowl ring on their fingers. They will ask themselves; what will it be like when we win the Super Bowl? What will the locker room look like after the game? They will see themselves celebrating in the locker room, being interviewed by the press, embracing their teammates—all before they ever tee it up. The Super Bowl will be clear, vivid, and precise. They will be so committed that nothing will stop them on their way to winning the Super Bowl.

How is it with you and your group? Do you write your goals down and stick them in a drawer? Or have you made your goals, your vision, an absolute part of your belief system? Can you see it? Can you taste it? Can you touch it? Can you smell it? Do you know what it sounds like? Have you made your vision such a vital part of your fiber, your being, that nothing, absolutely nothing will stop you from achieving it? Is your team united in its desire to win?

This is what a winning team looks like. It's not top-down. It's not somebody in a corner office, or an ivory tower, coming down here and telling us what to do. It's bottom-up—*people closest to the job know best how to do the job.* It's axiomatic.

Jack Welch, the widely admired CEO of General Electric, once described four types of leaders:

Type 1: delivers on commitments and shares the values of GE. The prospects for this person was "onward and upward."

Type 2: doesn't meet commitments and doesn't share GE's values. These people don't last long at GE.

Type 3: leaders miss commitments but share the values. These people get a second chance.

Type 4: leaders deliver on commitments, but don't share GE values. This individual forces performance out of people rather than inspires it. Welch stated that too often these types of leaders were tolerated because they "delivered."

Not any more, according to Welch. "In an environment where we must have every good idea from every man and woman in the organization, we cannot afford management styles that suppress and intimidate."

A group of hunters went to a game preserve to hunt birds. They told the owner what they wanted and mentioned they would need a dog. The owner said he had an excellent dog by the name of Coach, and he would cost $10. The hunters allowed that $10 was a lot of money for a dog. The owner said Coach was an excellent hunting dog. So off they went, and Coach was a great dog. He pointed the birds out, the hunters shot them, and Coach retrieved the birds without ruffling a feather. The hunters had such a great time, they returned the next week.

"We'd like Coach again," said one of the hunters. "That will be $20," the owner said. Reluctantly the hunters agreed and they had a second great experience. So they came back a third time. "We'd like Coach." "That will be $30." "$30?" "He's a good dog, he's in demand," said the owner. The hunters took Coach and had another great hunt.

So they came back a fourth time. "How much is Coach this week?" "$5" said the owner. "$5?" said the hunters, "Wait a minute, $10, $20, $30, now he's only $5—what's the story?" The owner said "Well, during the week someone took

*At too many compa-
nies, the boss shoots
the arrow of manage-
rial performance and
then hastily paints a
bulls-eye around the
spot where it lands.*
        —Warren Buffett

Coach out and they made a mistake. They called him 'Head' Coach. Now all he does is sit on his tail and bark at people."

There's no room for that kind of coach in today's high-performance organizations. The successful coach today gets everyone involved in defining the bulls-eye and gets everyone involved in hitting the bulls-eye. This is how you build *esprit de corps,* this is how you get people to really care about their work and the success of the organization.

Constant Reinforcement

There is at bottom only one problem in the world and this is its name. How does one break through? How does one get into the open? How does one burst the cocoon and become a butterfly?

—Thomas Mann

Have you ever wondered whether good coaches—good leaders—share a common attitude, or whether they have certain thought patterns in common? They do, and one of these thought patterns is: *The will to win, the will to achieve, goes dry and arid without constant reinforcement.*

Throughout history, the great leaders and prophets have experienced periods that could be described as their desert experience, when they've been confused, discouraged, and lost. Why, therefore, does it come as a surprise to us when as a coach or leader, we experience periods that are dry and arid, when we feel discouraged? Times of stress, when events are taking place so fast that we don't know the questions, much less have the answers.

Life is difficult! Life *is* difficult, but it doesn't have to be hard. Life comes to us in a series of challenges, and the attitude with which

The art of living is more like wrestling than dancing.
—Marcus Aerelius

we perceive these challenges and the mindset with which we prepare for them determines whether our lives are hard or whether our lives are rewarding.

Victor Frankl, a Jewish psychiatrist, spent World War II in a concentration camp; while in the camp he lost his wife, his child, and a manuscript that was his life's work. While in the camp, Frankl became fascinated with the question of why some people in the concentration camp quickly gave up and died and why others not only survived but some grew stronger. From his observations, Frankl concluded that it was how people chose to perceive their experience—their attitude was what made the difference. Frankl summed up his observations in his book, *Man's Search for Meaning*:

> *Everything can be taken from a man but one thing: the last of human freedoms, the ability to choose one's attitude in any given set of circumstances, to choose one's own way.*

The greatest discovery of my generation is that a human being can alter his life by altering his attitude.
—William James

What is the key to acquiring the kind of attitude that allows people to survive a concentration camp and allows you and me to live rewarding lives?

The key is *constant reinforcement.* A trap many of us fall into is that when we see or hear something that affects our attitude in a positive or constructive manner, we say to ourselves, "That's it, I've got it," then we go about our business. It doesn't work that way! We aren't made that way!

The truth that inspires and moves and encourages us wears many faces. It's been observed that of those things that move and inspire us—outside of the Bible, Emerson, and Shakespeare—very little has been written or expressed that's completely original. You have only to go to your favorite bookstore and check out the self-help section to understand there's more than one way to say basically the same thing.

But what may click for you, may leave me cold. Maybe you would rather listen to a tape, while I learn better reading a book. That's fine, but the critical point is that we need to spend time every day, every week listening to tapes, reading books, and surrounding ourselves with people we can learn from and grow with. What we're seeking with this constant reinforcement is that eventually we'll begin to internalize the thought processes of good coaches and leaders.

Have you ever wondered why successful coaches put so much emphasis on practice? They run the same plays over and over and over until the players can execute those plays in their sleep. And that's exactly what the coach wants! At the crucial moment of the big game, the coach can't have her players thinking about their next move. If the player has to think, it's too late: the game will pass right by him. Without thinking, players have to act and react appropriately. Their actions must be automatic. Their next move must be so internalized that it's instinctive and habitual.

It's the same for you and me. Things are happening so fast today we don't have time to stop and do an attitude check every time we're faced with a problem. If we have to think, we miss an opportunity. Our thought processes must be internalized through the constant reinforcement of reading books, listening to tapes, and associating with people with whom we can grow, so that we will appropriately respond to our next challenge, instinctively and intuitively.

During my father's years in Green Bay, the Packers usually featured a powerful offense. The entire offense was predicated upon the success of one play called the "Lombardi sweep." On this play, both guards pulled out of the line and with the fullback, led the halfback around the

The ideas I stand for are not mine. I borrowed them from Socrates. I swiped them from Chesterfield. I stole them from Jesus. And I put them in a book.
—Dale Carnegie

Books are the quietest and most consistent of friends; they are the most accessible and wisest of counselors, and they are the most patient of teachers.
—Charles W. Eliot

Nurture your mind with great thoughts. To believe in the heroic makes heroes.
—Benjamin Disraeli

Men acquire a particular quality by constantly acting in a particular way.
—Aristotle

Keep away from people who try to belittle your ambitions. Small people always do that, but the really great make you feel that you too, can become great.
—Mark Twain

We are what we repeatedly do. Excellence then is not an act, but a habit.

—Anonymous

end. This was the first play my father installed in training camp every year. The team practiced this play far more than any other, because this play had to be executed correctly for the Packer offense to succeed.

A defensive tackle for the Dallas Cowboys in those years told me that the week before the Cowboys played the Packers, the Cowboy defense worked almost exclusively on ways to stop the "Lombardi sweep." He told me that even though they practiced against the play all week, and even though they knew when it was going to be run and how the Packers would run it, the Cowboys still couldn't stop it.

So thoroughly had the Packers practiced this play, so intuitive were their reactions to the defensive challenges to the sweep, and so confident were they in their ability to execute it, that even when the opposition knew they were going to use the play, they still ran it successfully.

Asking questions is one important aspect of this process of constant reinforcement. Here's a question I came across in a publication called *Executive Excellence:* "Am I going to allow my life to be governed by daily activities, or do I choose to live my life in accordance with noble principles?"

The art and science of asking questions is the source of all knowledge.

—Dr. Adolf Berle

In other words, am I just reacting to life, or am I living my life in a proactive manner? Am I so busy putting out fires that I don't have time to start any? Am I allowing my life to be governed by outside forces, or am I choosing to live my life in accordance with decisions I'm making? Do I have important goals and dreams I am committed to, or am I creatively avoiding commitments by filling my life with daily activities?

In the absence of clearly defined goals, we are forced to concentrate on activity and ultimately become enslaved to it.

—Chuck Coonradt

Being a good coach is a process. It doesn't just happen—you can't leave it to chance. As a coach, you can orchestrate your team's performance. I'm not suggesting it's as easy as 1, 2, 3 or A, B, C—it doesn't work that way. This book strongly suggests, however, that if you desire to be a good coach and a good leader, then there is a certain body of knowledge—a certain fount of information—you need to have in your possession.

Good coaches know this information. They may not know they know it; we might call them "unconscious competents." But if you spend time with this process of constant reinforcement; reading and listening—this information will begin to become evident to you.

Winning is *choosing* to change, to grow, to improve performance. But before you can choose, you need to know that you have a *choice*. To know you have a choice, you need to know that you *can* grow and change. And to know that you can, you need to be in possession of the information you glean from this process of constant reinforcement.

And if it's a process, you had better have a plan. Your development plan as a coach or a leader should involve at least two components: experience and training or education. Experience is a great teacher. The problem is that we have to take the test before we learn the lesson. If only we could take our young people, open their heads, and pour in our experience. "If I only knew then what I know now," is a lament often repeated. But experience isn't enough. If it were, all of us with gray hair would be successful and fulfilled. We need to bring something to our experiences. That something is our power to observe and reflect. We must learn from each experience, from the people we associate with, and from the task itself. You observe and reflect, "What just happened, and how can I learn from this experience, and from the people associated with this experience?"

Einstein once defined insanity as doing the same thing over and over, but expecting the result to be different. He was describing the

There is a technique, a knack, for thinking, just as there is for doing other things. You are not wholly at the mercy of your thoughts, any more than they are you. They are a machine you can learn to operate.

—Alfred North Whitehead

A strong and well-constituted man digests his experiences (deeds and misdeeds all included) just as he digests his meats, even when he has some tough morsels to swallow.

—Friedrich Nietzsche

situation of not learning from our experiences.

Training and education complements and supplements this process of observation and reflection. An important aspect of your educational process should be constant reinforcement. Every week you should be spending time reading from the classics, autobiographies and biographies of outstanding people, essays on social responsibility and ethics, and self-improvement tapes and books. (See Suggested Reading list at end of book.) Eventually, through this plan of constant reinforcement you will begin to internalize the mindset and thought processes of a good coach, a good leader.

Good coaches learn from every experience through observation and reflection. They engage in formal training and education to complement their power to observe and reflect. They proceed on the basis that: *The will to win, the will to achieve, goes dry and arid without constant reinforcement.*

> *If you can't get enthusiastic about your work, it's time to become alarmed—something is wrong. Compete with yourself; set your teeth and dive into the job of breaking your own record. Enthusiasm must be nourished with new actions, new inspirations, new efforts and a new vision. It is one's own fault if his enthusiasm is gone; he has failed to feed it.*
>
> *—Papyrus*

In an information society, education is no mere amenity; it is the prime tool for growing people and profits.
—John Naisbitt and Patricia Aburdene

Leadership and learning are indispensable to each other.
—John F. Kennedy

Conclusion

After the cheers have died down and the stadium is empty, after the headlines have been written and after you are back in the quiet of your own room and the championship ring has been placed on the dresser and all the pomp and fanfare has faded, the enduring things that are left are: the dedication to excellence, the dedication to victory, and the dedication to doing with our lives the very best we can to make the world a better place in which to live.

—Vincent T. Lombardi

In the locker room, minutes before the Packers took the field to play the Oakland Raiders in Super Bowl II, my father called the players together and told them:

"It's very difficult for me to say anything. Anything I could say would be repetitious. This is our twenty-third game this year. I don't know anything else I could tell this team. Boys, I can only say this to you: Boys, you're a good football team. You are a proud football team. You are the world champions. You are champions of the National Football League, for the third time in a row, for the first time in the history of the National Football League. That's a great thing to be proud of. But let me just say this: All the glory, everything that you've had, everything that you've won is going to be small in comparison to winning this one. This is a great thing for you. You're the only team maybe in the history of the National Football League to ever have this opportunity to win the Super Bowl twice. Boys, I tell you I'd be so proud of that I just fill up with myself. I just get bigger and bigger and bigger. It's not going to come easy. This is a club that's gonna hit you. They're gonna try and hit you and you got to take it out of them. You got to be forty tigers out there. That's all. Just hit. Just run. Just block and just tackle. If you do that, there's no question what the answer's going to be in this ball game. Keep your poise. Keep your poise. You've faced them all. There's nothing they can show you out there you haven't faced a number of times. Right?"

This short locker room speech brings us full circle. Just like that letter to the players after the 1962 championship game, my father was once again reinforcing the players' self-esteem and self-confidence. Many of the things that have been emphasized in this book are contained in that short talk. Communicating the vision, the pay value in achieving the vision, training, sticking to the fundamentals, and mental toughness in the face of obstacles.

There's a lot made of the rings awarded to the team that wins the Super Bowl. The ring the Green Bay Packers wear for defeating the Oakland Raiders in Super Bowl II has three large diamonds across the face. The three diamonds signify the three consecutive world championships the Packers won, Super Bowl II being the third. The ring has dates and scores and opponents' names on it and on one side is the word "CHALLENGE." This signified the season-long challenge the Packers faced in trying to win three championships in a row and was the driving vision the Packers carried throughout the 1967 season. On the other side of the ring are the words "RUN TO WIN." This came from something my father said to the players the week before Super Bowl II as they prepared to play the Raiders. My father quoted a passage of the Bible to the players. He quoted St. Paul as saying:

> *Do you know that all who run in a race, all indeed run. But only one receives the prize. So run to win.*
>
> **—I Corinthians 9:24**

What I believe St. Paul might have been saying and what my father might have been repeating, is that the thing that differentiates between or among us as teams and as individuals is not a lack of strength, not a lack of education, but a lack of *will*. For it's *character*, not power, not knowledge, that is our greatest prize.

It's character—with its attributes of courage and discipline and loyalty and sacrifice—that is not only the thing that differentiates between or among us, it's the difference between the great teams and the also-rans.

By great, I don't mean you've done something big and you have your name in the newspapers. Greatness isn't talent. Greatness is not ability. Rather, greatness is the willingness and the commitment and the discipline to use the talent and the ability you possess to the fullest.

Are you the best husband you can be? If you are, you are great. The best wife? If you are, you are great. The best mother, the best father? If you are, you are great. The best leader, the best

Champions aren't made in gyms. Champions are made from something they have deep inside of them—a desire, a dream, a vision. They have to have lasting stamina, they have to be a little faster, they have to have skill and the will. But the will must be stronger than the skill.
—Muhammad Ali

Everyone has talent. What is rare is the courage to follow the talent to the dark place where it leads.
—Erica Jong

Though the talents you possess may appear to be average or less, use them anyway. The woods would be very silent indeed if no birds sang except the very best.

—Unknown

coach? If you are, you are great.

And don't believe anything you read in the magazines or the newspapers, and please don't believe anything you see on television that tells you anything different. **You are great!**

My father once said, *"I firmly believe that any man's finest hour, the greatest fulfillment of all that he holds dear; is that moment, when he has worked his heart out in a good cause and lies exhausted on the field of battle, victorious."* It would be my very sincere hope that each and every one of you will have the good fortune my father had and all good coaches and leaders have. That is, to have a good cause for which to work your heart out. If you have that good cause, or when you find it, *"Run to win."*

Life itself is a race, marked by a start, and a finish. It is what we learn during the race, and how we apply it, that determines whether our participation has had a particular value. If we learn from each success, and each failure, and improve ourselves through this process, then, at the end, we will have fulfilled our potential and performed well.

—Unknown

Suggested Reading

A Better World, a Better You. Louis E. Tice with Alan Steinberg. Englewood Cliffs, NJ: Prentice Hall, 1989.

Flow. Mihaly Csikszentmihalyi. New York: Harper & Row, 1990.

From Confucius to Oz. Vernon Crawford. New York: Berkeley Books, 1989.

Future Edge. Joel Arthur Barker. New York: William Morrow and Company, 1992.

The Game of Work. Charles A. Coonradt with Lee Nelson. Salt Lake City: Deseret Book Company, 1984.

Leadership is an Art. Max DePree. New York: Doubleday, 1989.

Leadership Secrets of Attila the Hun. Wess Roberts, Ph.D. New York: Warner Books, 1990.

Learned Optimism. Martin E. P. Seligman, Ph.D. New York: Simon & Schuster, 1990.

Man's Search for Meaning. Viktor E. Frankl. New York: Washington Square Press, 1959.

Mentally Tough. Dr. James E. Loehr and Peter J. McLaughlin. New York: M. Evans and Company, 1986.

Peak Performers. Charles Garfield. New York: Avon Books, 1986.

Principle-Centered Leadership. Stephen R. Covey. New York: Summit Books, 1990.

Psycho-Cybernetics. Maxwell Maltz, M.D. Englewood Cliffs, NJ: Prentice Hall, 1960.

The 7 Habits of Highly Effective People. Stephen R. Covey. New York: Simon & Schuster, 1989.

Toughness Training for Life. James E. Loehr, Ed.D. New York: Penguin Books, 1993.

Index

Give the Gift of Teamwork to Your Friends and Colleagues

CHECK YOUR LEADING BOOKSTORE OR ORDER BELOW

☐ **YES**, I want ____ copies of *Coaching for Teamwork* at $14.95 each, plus $3 shipping per book (WA residents please add $1.23 state sales tax per book). Canadian orders must be accompanied by a postal money order in U.S. funds. Allow 15 days for delivery.

☐ **YES**, I am interested in having Vince Lombardi speak or give a seminar to my company, association, school, or organization. Please send information.

My check or money order for $_____ is enclosed.

Name _____ Phone _____

Organization _____

Address _____

City/State/Zip _____

Please make your check payable to:

Reinforcement Press
2820 122nd Place NE
Bellevue, WA 98005
Fax: (206) 882-1648

Give the Gift of Teamwork to Your Friends and Colleagues

CHECK YOUR LEADING BOOKSTORE OR ORDER BELOW

☐ **YES**, I want _____ copies of *Coaching for Teamwork* at $14.95 each, plus $3 shipping per book (WA residents please add $1.23 state sales tax per book). Canadian orders must be accompanied by a postal money order in U.S. funds. Allow 15 days for delivery.

☐ **YES**, I am interested in having Vince Lombardi speak or give a seminar to my company, association, school, or organization. Please send information.

My check or money order for $_____ is enclosed.

Name _____ Phone _____

Organization _____

Address _____

City/State/Zip _____

Please make your check payable to:

Reinforcement Press
2820 122nd Place NE
Bellevue, WA 98005
Fax: (206) 882-1648